The Cambridge Introduction to
F. Scott Fitzgerald

Although F. Scott Fitzgerald remains one of the most recognizable literary figures of the twentieth century, his legendary life – including his tempestuous romance with his wife and muse Zelda – continues to overshadow his art. However glamorous his image as the poet laureate of the 1920s, he was first and foremost a great writer with a gift for fluid, elegant prose. This introduction reminds readers why Fitzgerald deserves his preeminent place in literary history. It discusses not only his best-known works, *The Great Gatsby* (1925) and *Tender Is the Night* (1934), but the full scope of his output, including his other novels and his short stories. This book introduces new readers and students of Fitzgerald to his trademark themes, his memorable characters, his significant plots, the literary modes and genres from which he borrowed, and his inimitable style.

KIRK CURNUTT is Professor of English at Troy University-Montgomery. He is vice president of the International F. Scott Fitzgerald Society, managing editor of the *F. Scott Fitzgerald Review* and a board member of the Scott and Zelda Fitzgerald Museum in Montgomery, Alabama.

Cambridge Introductions to Literature

This series is designed to introduce students to key topics and authors.
Accessible and lively, these introductions will also appeal to readers who
want to broaden their understanding of the books and authors they enjoy.

- Ideal for students, teachers, and lecturers
- Concise, yet packed with essential information
- Key suggestions for further reading

Titles in this series:

The Cambridge Introduction to
F. Scott Fitzgerald

KIRK CURNUTT

CAMBRIDGE
UNIVERSITY PRESS

CAMBRIDGE UNIVERSITY PRESS
Cambridge, New York, Melbourne, Madrid, Cape Town, Singapore, São Paulo

Cambridge University Press
The Edinburgh Building, Cambridge CB2 8RU, UK

Published in the United States of America by Cambridge University Press, New York

www.cambridge.org
Information on this title: www.cambridge.org/9780521676007

First published 2007

Printed in the United Kingdom at the University Press, Cambridge

A catalogue record for this publication is available from the British Library

Library of Congress Cataloguing in Publication data
Curnutt, Kirk, 1964–
The Cambridge introduction to F. Scott Fitzgerald / Kirk Curnutt.
  p. cm. – (Cambridge introductions to literature)
Includes bibliographical references and index.
ISBN-13: 978-0-521-85909-7
ISBN-10: 0-521-85909-3
ISBN-13: 978-0-521-67600-7 (pbk)
ISBN-10: 0-521-67600-2 (pbk)
1. Fitzgerald, F. Scott (Francis Scott), 1896–1940 – Criticism and interpretation.
I. Title. II. Series.
PS3511.I9Z584   2007
813′.52 – dc22
2006032443

ISBN 978-0-521-85909-7 hardback
ISBN 978-0-521-67600-7 paperback

Contents

Preface

This study introduces F. Scott Fitzgerald to two very different audiences: those who possess only a passing familiarity with his life and work, and those who already know him thoroughly. For the former group – whether students or general readers – my overviews of his biography, his oeuvre, his historical context, and his critical reception provide the basic information necessary for appreciating his literary legacy. While assembling the essential details, I also wish to impart a working knowledge of how they have been previously presented so that newcomers may understand why their recitation has reduced some facts to commonplaces while others remain relatively ignored.

This latter goal further suggests why I simultaneously address a second readership of fellow aficionados, many of whom, frankly, are far more distinguished scholars than I: I firmly believe that Fitzgerald is undergoing the kind of critical makeover that writers of his stature periodically require to prevent their reputations from fossilizing. Throughout the seven decades since the author of *The Great Gatsby* was posthumously rehabilitated, scholars have demonstrated a talent for reinvigorating interest in him. The 1990s and 2000s have proved an especially fertile period, with the result that to describe Fitzgerald as a leading literary encyclopedia does seems lamentably reductive: "Widely considered the literary spokesman of the 'jazz age' . . . Part of the interest of his work derives from the fact that the mad, gin-drinking, morally and spiritually bankrupt men and women he wrote about led lives that closely resembled his own."[1] In attempting to scrape away such barnacles of cliché, the present volume reflects devotees' concerted efforts to provide recent initiates and long-time admirers alike a dimensioned appreciation of his output.

Accomplishing this goal justifies what readers may find a surprising structural decision on my part: in analyzing Fitzgerald's work in my central chapter, "Works," I eschew chronology in favor of a topical organization that allows me to assess themes, characters, and genres free of any prejudicial presumptions about a piece's place in the trajectory of his career. The "developmental model" of literary analysis, I contend, has limited our understanding of Fitzgerald. Although few would disagree that he "peaked" in 1925 with *The Great Gatsby*, that conviction inevitably taints the discussion of other efforts by inviting us to look for flaws that can be attributed to whatever personal and/or professional valley he may have been suffering at a particular moment. A non-chronological approach, by contrast, allows us to assess his texts according to their own criteria rather than that of his best-known work. It discourages us from reading his debut novel, *This Side of Paradise* (1920), for the greatness it might foreshadow instead of achieve, for example, and to rediscover a story like "Family in the Wind" (1932) that is neglected simply because it does not reinforce the legend. Organizing by category instead of timeline has the additional benefit of highlighting the continuity of authorial interests. It invites us to compare, for example, Jay Gatsby to Monroe Stahr, the hero of Fitzgerald's final, uncompleted novel, *The Last Tycoon* (1941), two characters not often discussed in the same breath simply because fifteen years separate their conception.[2]

My views on Fitzgerald reflect the influence of several mentors to whom I am indebted: Ruth Prigozy, Jackson R. Bryer, J. Gerald Kennedy, Scott Donaldson, Ronald Berman, Milton R. Stern, Linda Wagner-Martin, James L. W. West III, and Matthew J. Bruccoli. Special thanks as well to James H. Meredith, William Blazek, Gail D. Sinclair, Cathy W. Barks, Heidi Kunz, Michael K. Glenday, Susan Wanlass, and many, many more; the editorial board of the *F. Scott Fitzgerald Review*; the board of directors of the Scott and Zelda Fitzgerald Museum in Montgomery, Alabama; and the membership of the International Fitzgerald Society, whose enthusiasm is contagious.

Introduction

Azar Nafisi's memoir, *Reading Lolita in Tehran* (2003), tells the story of an Islamic woman teaching Western classics in Iran between 1979, when Muslim fundamentalists under the Ayatollah Khomeini seized control of the country, and 1997, when Nafisi emigrated to America. In addition to Henry James's *Washington Square* (1881), Jane Austen's *Pride and Prejudice* (1813), and the Vladimir Nabokov novel cited in her title, her syllabus includes F. Scott Fitzgerald's *The Great Gatsby* (1925), which she assigns shortly after militants storm the US embassy on November 4, 1979, initiating a 444-day hostage crisis. Given the roiling anti-Americanism that Khomeini fomented, it is not surprising to learn that some of Nafisi's students at the University of Tehran attack this quintessentially American novel. More intriguing is how deeply – not to mention how differently – others are affected by the tale of the enigmatic millionaire whose unlikely presence in the ritzy enclaves of Long Island Sound upends old-money notions of *noblesse oblige*. One colleague risks being censured as "anti-revolutionary" for dubbing himself "Little Great Gatsby" because he owns a swimming pool. A fiery zealot decides that the only commendable character is George Wilson, the cuckolded garage owner who murders Jay Gatsby in the mistaken belief that he is responsible for the death of Wilson's wife, Myrtle; as "the genuine symbol of the oppressed, in the land of . . . the Great Satan," Wilson serves as the smiting "hand of God," meting divine justice to Fitzgerald's decadent materialists.[1] Offended by this religious rhetoric, a young woman argues that *Gatsby* is about the illusoriness of aspiration, a theme that to her reveals more about fallibility than all the sanctimonious talk of right and wrong.

In a risky move Nafisi invites her class to stage a mock trial meant to mimic (if not parody) the rampant public trials of state enemies. The goal is to decide not only *The Great Gatsby*'s defining theme but the purpose of literature itself. Called to defend Fitzgerald, the embattled instructor refutes the prosecution's claim that the plot is amoral because it centers upon an adulterous relationship (a charge that, perhaps unbeknownst to Nafisi, was leveled by some early reviewers):

> You don't read *Gatsby* to learn whether adultery is good or bad but to
> learn about how complicated issues such as adultery and fidelity and
> marriage are. A great novel heightens your senses and sensitivity to the
> complexities of life and of individuals, and prevents you from the
> self-righteousness that sees morality in fixed formulas about good and
> evil. (133)

As a fellow professor, I find it difficult to read Nafisi's story without a twinge
of envy, for her students' debate makes palpable something that we who eke out
our livings in the literature classroom desperately want to believe: because art
spurs critical thinking, and because societies regardless of political persuasion
will seek to suppress the potentially dangerous knowledge it circulates, educa-
tors have a moral duty to expose students to its prohibited content, regardless
of the costs of our advocacy. Despite its Middle Eastern setting, *Reading Lolita
in Tehran* belongs to a popular genre that dramatizes this contention. Including both novels (Muriel Spark's *The Prime of Miss Jean Brodie*, 1962) and films
(the Robin Williams vehicle *Dead Poets Society*, 1989), these are narratives in
which brave teachers suffer the slings and arrows of small-minded administra-
tors and parents who object to any challenging of inherited moralities. Nafisi's
witness-stand denunciation of "fixed formulas" is actually a defining plot point
of the genre, which climaxes with the protagonist standing up to a repressive
governing body by delivering a rousing panegyric on art's capacity to compel
young people to new realms of insight.

Alas, one of the first things I discovered about teaching is that opportunities
to speechify on literature's uplift are actually few and far between. For nearly
a decade and a half now, I have worked at a "non-traditional" university, the
kind that in a less sensitive era was condescendingly referred to as a "night
school." Our 4,500 students are mostly working adults, many of them United
States Air Force enlistees. When I joined the faculty in 1993 – as green and naïve
as any freshly minted PhD beginning his first "real" job at twenty-eight could
possibly be – the average age was thirty-three. Over the years, that number
has dropped to twenty-six as economic downturns continue to force a higher
proportion of recent high school graduates into the full-time labor force. What
has not changed is the prevailing suspicion that literature is an elitist luxury
with little relevance outside of the small circle of "experts" privy to its occult
meanings. I can appreciate my students' adverse opinion of it because I am
sympathetic to the pressures they must negotiate even to remain in school;
there is nothing more eye-opening than having a 47-year-old African-American
woman breakdown during a research paper consultation because she fears her
employer is plotting a round of lay-offs, or to have a 27-year-old staff sergeant

ask to complete the class after the semester because his unit has been deployed to Baghdad.

Because education on my campus is often a third priority behind work and family commitments, I find myself struggling to convince classes that literature can have real-world applications and that assigned readings can be more than mere hoops hopped through on the way to a degree. On bad days I defensively console myself by insisting that my advocacy is a necessary and perhaps even noble endeavor, but even on the good ones I am aware that it is hardly the stuff of riveting drama. The reason why memoirs like Nafisi's or Roberta Huntley's *The Hemingway Book Club of Kosovo* (also 2003), which substitutes *The Old Man and the Sea* (1952) for *The Great Gatsby*, have proved so popular is that they make imminent the consequences of their Socratic insistence that literature will redeem the unexamined life. Their war-torn settings and the repressive regimes they oppose lend urgency to their literary purpose, and urgency is something that, for all the overhyped talk of the culture wars dividing the groves of academe, is not always easy to generate in the classroom. The simple reality is that few teachers like me will ever be commanded to drink the hemlock in the name of our pedagogical imperatives. The question likely put to most of us is not the one Nafisi's students pose when she encourages them to explore the mythic nature of Gatsby's love for Daisy Fay Buchanan: "What use is love in this world we live in?" (110). Instead, we face ones that are far more formidable impediments, such as I recently did when I encountered a forty-year-old business major at a local watering hole who was just pickled enough to protest about his curricular requirements: "Why do they make me take your class, anyway?"

Rather than resent such questions, I believe in taking up their gauntlet. In the spirit of Nafisi, the present volume is an invitation to explore a variation on her class's concern: what use is F. Scott Fitzgerald in this world we live in? The answer might seem self-evident, for in the popular culture Fitzgerald remains one of America's most recognizable literary icons, his physiognomy as prominent on the Mt Rushmore of national belletrists as Edgar Allan Poe, Mark Twain, and Ernest Hemingway. Since the 1940s, when he was posthumously reclaimed from obscurity, the story of his rise to renown in the 1920s, his declining popularity in the 1930s, his alcoholism, and his doomed romance with his wife and muse Zelda Sayre has been kept alive through biographies and *romans à clef*, television documentaries and dramatizations, dour kitchen-sink melodramas and glitzy Broadway-style musicals. *The Great Gatsby*, his best-known novel, likewise long ago entered the public vernacular, inspiring movies, operas, and ballets while lending its dapper imprimatur to bars, streets, clothing lines, planned communities, and even, in the 1970s, sugar packets.[2] So assured is his status that to undermine it dissenters must resort to calumny: "Fitzgerald was a bad writer who has somehow gained the reputation of a good one," reads a throwaway line in a recent biography of Arnold Rothstein, the New York mobster who inspired *Gatsby*'s shadowy Meyer Wolfshiem.[3] Such statements smack of flippant contrarianism rather than reasoned argumentation, and they rarely rise above the persuasiveness of a minority opinion.

A far greater threat to Fitzgerald's prominence is that the qualities sustaining it – elegant sophistication and the pathos of personal tragedy – rarely resonate with students like mine. This is frustrating, given that I live in Montgomery, Alabama, one of the three or four most influential sites in the writer's biography. It was here, after all, that Scott first met Zelda in 1918, and certain parts of the city – which Fitzgerald dubbed "Tarleton, Georgia" in his fiction – still resonate with their fabled romance. Discussing "The Ice Palace" (1920), for example, I like to note that our local Oakwood Cemetery – a popular tourist attraction, thanks to its most famous occupant, Hank Williams – is the place where Sally Carrol Happer's mellifluous meditation on Southern mutability takes place. Other significant locales include Taylor Field (now Maxwell Air Force Base, where many of my military students work), the former Elite Restaurant (one block east of our campus), Pleasant Avenue (where Scott courted Zelda at her parents' house), Oak Park (where Zelda swam), the remnants of Camp Sheridan north of town (where Scott was barracked), and many others. Occasionally, I even round up students and take them to 919 Felder Avenue, where the Fitzgeralds wintered in 1931–2 shortly after Zelda was released from the first of her many sanitarium stays. Since 1987, this address has been home to the Scott and Zelda Fitzgerald Museum Association, which holds the distinction of operating the only house and grounds the couple ever lived in that is open to the public. Yet, as much as I try to impress upon students their good fortune at studying Fitzgerald in an environment that so shaped his fiction, our proximity to this history does surprisingly little to ignite their enthusiasm.

Another reason I find this lack of interest frustrating is that I have vivid memories of my own undergraduate introduction to Fitzgerald in 1985 as a sophomore at the University of Missouri-Columbia. Back then, it was not rare to encounter campus beaux scouring *All the Sad Young Men* (1926) for a line to impress their ladyloves, or coeds showing off the paper dolls they had crafted after perusing an outrageously priced copy of the Fitzgeralds' scrapbooks, *The Romantic Egoists* (1973), in a used-book store. Young women toted paperback copies of Nancy Milford's 1970 biography *Zelda* (usually borrowed from their mothers) to signal the wild, irrepressible personae they cultivated, and fliers featured Art Deco designs that evoked the covers of *The Beautiful and*

Damned (1922) and *Tender Is the Night* (1934). Occasionally, word of house parties requiring 1920s attire made the rounds, and the vintage-clothing outlets would be chockfull of aspiring revelers searching for affordable (i.e., used) tuxedo jackets and flapper dresses. More important, the more literary sorts strove to demonstrate their affinity with Fitzgerald's vibrancy and poignancy; to discourse on the beauty of the mascara tear that runs down a young woman's cheek in *Gatsby*'s third chapter was to prove that, like the titular hero himself, one possessed a "heightened sensitivity to the promises of life."[4]

I assume such things still happen, though I suspect they are limited to that rather rarefied world of the traditional college English department, where the connection between life and literature needs no explication. As for my students, I find the reasons why they are not predisposed to share my passion for Fitzgerald both revelatory and instructive. For starters, for a working- and lower-middle-class population, the elite world of country clubs, debutante parties, and mansions in which the majority of his work is set can seem dubiously snobbish, preppy, and even effete. His *haut bourgeois* fixation with prestige and social distinction strikes them as aristocratic rather than democratic, which offends their proletarian sympathies. African-American students in particular find little reason to relate to him when contemporaries such as Langston Hughes and Zora Neale Hurston speak more directly to their heritage. (I am proud to report that my campus is the most integrated of all Alabama colleges, with nearly thirty percent of our population composed of African-American women. Even in the twenty-first century, that is no mean feat in a Southern state with such a tortured racial history.) Interestingly, age proves as decisive a barrier as class and race. Fitzgerald's preoccupation with youth often strikes our post-thirty population as irredeemably adolescent. Our teens and twentysomethings, by contrast, find him irredeemably antiquated, especially in light of the casual bagginess that hip-hop has brought to their fashion and slang. Bred in a landscape of digital celerity in which the past appears to have little demonstrable connection to the here and now, this age group frankly considers the 1920s Jazz Age as remote as the Paleozoic era. A handful of my undergraduates may emulate the prose and personae of Hemingway, Jack Kerouac, or Sylvia Plath, but that is because these authors' expatriate forays, pharmaceutical experimentation, and raw adolescent anger are not quite so foreign to their maturation experiences as the whimsy of "The Ice Palace" or the lachrymose glitter of *The Great Gatsby*. Finally, there is the problem of Fitzgerald's romanticism, whose ornate, formal volubility alienates classes regardless of age or ethnicity. While never as willfully obscure as such "High Modernists" as James Joyce, Ezra Pound, or Gertrude Stein, Fitzgerald nevertheless wrote in a passionate, lyrical style whose emotional vulnerability is at odds with the insouciant irony that has dominated literary expression since the mid-1970s. Such obstacles demonstrate why teachers can never presume Fitzgerald's importance; classroom discussions must recognize student likes and dislikes in order to transcend them. Otherwise, the experience of reading will never rise above the drudgery of an assignment.

An essential issue for debate within this dialogue, I would further add, is the meaning of literary relevance itself. As I often admit to classes, I am not always certain that I know the line between trying to interest them in Fitzgerald and pandering to their interests. I talk openly of how, while I want to facilitate emotional connections with his work, I also hope to challenge the criteria determining students' personal likes and dislikes – much as learning from the reasons for their ambivalence toward him teaches me to interrogate mine. One of my favorite initial reactions to *The Great Gatsby* provides an excellent entry into this discussion: "I couldn't get into it," a class member will say, by which he or she usually means, "This work had no personal relevance to me." Classes are sometimes taken aback by my standard response: "Why should a work have to be *personally* relevant to you to be meaningful? Might there not be things worth learning about Fitzgerald and his place in American literature that have no direct bearing on your interests?"

My question is as useful as it is provocative because it allows us to debate the pros and cons of personal response, which is the interpretive strategy in which they and I alike were first trained. Influenced by the anti-institutionalism of the 1960s, this pedagogy emerged out of the then-fledgling field of composition studies, popularized by theorists such as Peter Elbow and Donald J. Murray. In general terms, personal-response writing insists that literary interpretation is a tool for empowering us to cultivate self-awareness and shape individual subjectivity, aims often celebrated under the vaguely self-help-sounding umbrella phrase "finding one's voice." By the mid-1970s, this approach proved wildly popular in literature classrooms because it provided a method for engaging students unenthused by the prospect of explicating symbols and delineating themes. When I introduce this background during discussion periods, I usually enjoy a rewarding "Aha!" moment, one of those instances when students recognize the relevance of the point I invite them to ponder. That "Aha!" typically evaporates when I posit a more controversial idea: that interpretation performs the equally valuable service of encouraging a *loss* of self as well as its discovery. As I try to convey to students who cling a little too furiously to the "couldn't get into it" rationale, at least some relaxing of the "I"'s imperious tendency to view the world as a narrow reflection of itself is necessary if the true goal of education is to promote critical reflection. Such is Nafisi's aim, in fact, when she discourages her class from the "self-righteousness that sees morality in fixed formulas about good and evil." As she argues from the witness stand:

> A good novel is one that shows the complexity of individuals, and creates enough space for all these characters to have a voice; in this way is a novel called democratic – not that it advocates democracy but that by nature it is so. Empathy lies at the heart of *Gatsby*, like so many other great novels – the biggest sin is to be blind to others' problems and pains. Not seeing them means denying their existence. (132)

Empathy is an excellent if unlikely byproduct of discussing relevance: it suggests the necessity of readers stepping beyond their individual enthusiasms to appreciate the significance of "others' problems and pains" and acknowledge the larger world of experience surrounding them. Again, this imperative applies to teachers as much as students; it is a prerogative that we must demonstrate we pursue instead of simply preach. Otherwise, we cheapen the value of the intellectual capital we seek to cultivate by passively resenting our supposed irrelevance to "real" life rather than actively creating its pertinence.

To return to our defining question then: what use is F. Scott Fitzgerald in this world we live in? As the chapters that follow demonstrate, he has much to teach us about issues of ongoing valence, in regard to both literature and, more broadly, culture – and not merely American culture, either, as *Reading Lolita in Tehran* again demonstrates. Appreciating his relevance, however, requires rescuing him from a central misperception that has tainted his reputation. The long-held belief that he was ultimately a "failed" writer because his personal problems impeded his productivity and because he had fallen out of favor by the time of his December 21, 1940, death begs the question of why artists are compelling only when their lives can be deemed "tragic" and their promise "unfulfilled." Contemporaries such as Eugene O'Neill, William Saroyan, and John Steinbeck suffered comparable ups and downs, yet their biographies exert little sway over the popular imagination. The reason is simple: their stories cannot be reduced to a parable as readily as Fitzgerald's can. Thanks to his career trajectory – early, intense success followed by a long downward spiral – he has come to serve as our literary Icarus, the golden boy whose ambition and ingenuity took him too close to the sun, melting the wings of his talent. (The Icarus motif is especially appropriate when we remember Hemingway's description of Fitzgerald's "butterfly wings" in *A Moveable Feast* [1964]: "He became conscious of his damaged wings and of their construction and he learned to think and could not fly any more because the love of flight was gone and he could only remember when it had been effortless.")[5] Failure is the essential component of his legend because, without it, he could not symbolize the lesson we have wanted to derive from his example – namely, that however hard we beat against our limitations, our weaknesses humble our gifts, and we are forced to abide in a world incommensurate with the capacities of imagination.

However appealing the Icarus myth, it distorts and distracts. It is responsible for the presumption that Fitzgerald produced only one truly "great" novel (*Gatsby*, of course), while the rest of his oeuvre is flawed and sloppy. For decades, this presumption proved particularly damaging to *Tender Is the Night*, whose perceived imperfections (a discursive narrative structure and inconsistent point of view) were attributed to the nine years it took to complete. Fitzgerald's early novels, *This Side of Paradise* (1920) and *The Beautiful and Damned*, suffer the even more degrading fate of being dismissed as "juvenile" or "apprentice" efforts. The myth has also caused a severe underestimation of Fitzgerald's short fiction. To tease out the Icarus parallel, we might say that the sun responsible for the waning of his literary wax was the *Saturday Evening Post*, that mass-circulation paragon of middle-class respectability whose generous remuneration led him to squander his energies on silly love stories. Fitzgerald bears much responsibility for this commonplace. In a well-known 1929 letter to Hemingway, he described himself as an "old whore" whom the *Post* now paid "$4000. a screw."[6] The metaphor does a vast injustice to the sixty-five stories he sold to the *Post* from 1920 to 1937, as well as the additional 100 he published elsewhere. Readers who encounter "Winter Dreams" (1922) or "Babylon Revisited" (1931) in a literary anthology will have a hard time understanding just how these classics represent a prostitution of talent. Even as one begins to recognize the plot formulae within lesser works, there remains an undisputable level of craftsmanship. Moreover, dismissing Fitzgerald's stories as slick contrivances ignores the range of genre, style, and technique with which he experimented. Some of his best stories are comedies of manners ("Bernice Bobs Her Hair," 1920), while others are fantasies ("The Diamond as Big as the Ritz," 1922) and still others acute social commentaries ("May Day," 1920). Once we remove the stigma of the "commercial" from them, we recognize that his contributions to the short story rank him among such certified masters as James, William Faulkner, and, of course, Hemingway.

The obligatorily "tragic" interpretation of Fitzgerald's life also overlooks the fact that he was adept at comedy as well as tragedy. Early non-fiction pieces such as "The Cruise of the Rolling Junk" and "How to Live on $36,000 a Year" (both 1924) are as funny as anything by the Algonquin wits. Indeed, while the work of George S. Kaufman or Alexander Woollcott has aged poorly, these cheeky essays remain fresh because of Fitzgerald's self-deprecation, which allowed him to satirize the excesses of the Jazz Age by ribbing his and Zelda's own reputation as impulsive spendthrifts. There is also a great deal of humor in his fiction, whether in the coy repartee of flapper stories like "The Offshore Pirate" (1920) or in the skewering caricatures of wannabe artists such as Chester McKee in *The Great Gatsby* and Albert McKisco in *Tender Is the Night*. And while the disappointments of the 1930s disinclined Fitzgerald from exercising this side of his genius, his Pat Hobby stories pungently lampoon Hollywood narcissism and amorality. This is not to say that Fitzgerald's comedic instincts were unimpeachable; there is no more painful read in his canon than *The Vegetable*, his disastrous 1923 foray into theatrical farce. Nevertheless, wryness was as natural to his temperament as the melancholy for which he is remembered.

Once these misconceptions are corrected, several themes in Fitzgerald's life and works reveal their pertinence. His struggle for critical acknowledgment dramatizes the difficulty that "popular" authors face when trying to build reputations as "serious" artists. His signature storyline of middle-class beaux pursuing rich girls exposes sex roles and social barriers that remain entrenched in the twenty-first century. And while his flappers may seem quaint throwbacks to a time when bobbed hair and bared legs were sufficiently rebellious to shock elders, their struggle to break the repressive bonds of propriety in a culture that at once stigmatized and exploited female sexuality is no different from the dilemmas that contemporary women face. Moreover, the tendency of Fitzgerald's protagonists to succumb to dissipation and prodigality points to the consequences of glamorizing self-indulgence and irresponsibility, as Western popular culture has done since the Jazz Age. Finally, Fitzgerald's greatest legacy, his gift for evoking loss in fluid, aching strokes of prose, makes him an excellent resource for analyzing the affective power of metaphors, imagery, and other figures of speech.

Finally, although rarely recognized for his political substance, Fitzgerald helps us to appreciate both the appeal and the perils of nationalism, which ignited two world wars during his lifetime and continues (along with religious fundamentalism) to augur instability in our own. There is no hoarier cliché in Fitzgerald studies than the claim that his work addresses the "American Dream," though whether he celebrates or critiques it is disputable. Suffice it to say that few writers evoke the paradoxes of "America" as deftly as he does in *Gatsby* and short stories such as "The Swimmers" (1929). In the concluding paragraph of this unappreciated piece, Fitzgerald conveys patriotism and provincialism

simultaneously as Henry Clay Marston meditates on the metaphorical reso-
nance of his homeland:

> He had a sense of overwhelming gratitude and of gladness that America
> was there, that under the ugly debris of industry the rich land still
> pushed up, incorrigibly lavish and fertile, and that in the heart of the
> leaderless people the old generosities and devotions fought on, breaking
> out sometimes in fanaticism and excess but indomitable and
> undefeated . . . France was a land, England was a people, but America,
> having about it still that quality of the idea, was harder to utter – it was
> the graves at Shiloh and the tired, drawn, nervous faces of its great men,
> and the country boys dying in the Argonne for a phrase that was empty
> before their bodies withered. It was a willingness of the heart.[7]

Out of context, the passage seems to endorse the American belief that its
ideals are exportable models of global liberty; it invokes that "shining city on
a hill" rhetoric that excites so much resentment in the non-Western world.
One can only imagine how Nafisi's militant students would react. They would
likely point out that, up until 1979, the main Iranian beneficiary of American
"willingness" was Shah Mohammed Reza Pahlavi, whose US-backed regime
was toppled by the Khomeini revolution. Nafisi would not fail to challenge
this reading, however. She would note that Marston commends American
"generosities" from the deck of a ship bound for France, where he will permanently settle. What sends Marston back to Europe is the gap between the
promise of America and its reality. (For partisans tempted to denounce the
story as anti-American, it is worth remembering that part of the source of his
unhappiness in America is his unfaithful wife, who happens to be . . . *French*.
Complexities abound.) Despite Marston's disappointment, he is far from rejecting "America" – rather, the disparity makes him value his country all the more
as a symbol. Nafisi might then point out that similar discrepancies mark all
emblems. The ability to accept the inevitable gap between the real and the ideal
is what separates the critical thinker from the ideologue, the true intellectual
from the apparatchik and apologist. She implies as much in her memoir's most
striking moment, in which she compares the failure of Gatsby's dream to those
that doomed the Iranian revolution to replace the Shah's monarchical abuses
with Khomeini's theocratic ones:

> What we in Iran had in common with Fitzgerald was this dream that
> became our obsession and overtook our reality, this terrible, beautiful
> dream, impossible in its actualization, for which any amount of violence
> might be justified or forgiven . . . He wanted to fulfill his dream by
> repeating the past, and to the end he discovered that the past was dead,

the present a sham, and there was no future. Was this not similar to our revolution, which had come in the name of our collective past and had wrecked our lives in the name of a dream?   (144)

Such paragraphs offer reason enough to value Fitzgerald: his work transcends its milieu to lend insight into an entirely foreign historical situation. The more we encourage students to pry behind the 1920s façade, the more likely it is that they, like Nafisi's, will recognize that his writings are not period pieces but timely representations of human yearning.

Life

"The history of my life is the history of the struggle between an overwhelming urge to write and a combination of circumstances bent on keeping me from it," Fitzgerald once admitted.[1] Few writers have ever penned as apt an epitaph. From an early age – the quotation appeared in the *Saturday Evening Post* on September 18, 1920, a week before its author turned twenty-four – he recognized that literary accomplishment would require a dextrous balancing of the events inspiring his fiction and the hard work of actually producing it. The ledger in which he assessed his annual output reveals how poorly he felt he managed the task: June 1925 was a month of "1000 parties and no work," while 1928–9 was written off as "no real progress in any way," and March 1936 was notable only for "work going badly."[2] Such rebukes were not merely a private habit; Fitzgerald frequently criticized himself in print, mourning what "I might have been and done" were his talents not "lost, spent, gone, dissipated, unrecapturable."[3] Unfortunately, because he was so open about his perceived incapacities, after 1925 he became as famous for the "combination of circumstances" hampering his prolificacy as for the classics he did complete. Retellings of his life story often sensationalize these impediments – his precarious finances, marital instability, alcoholism, and Zelda's mental illness – forgetting that Fitzgerald was productive both *in spite* and *because of* them. His tribulations were the source material that allowed him to pursue the larger literary goal of measuring the moral implications of his era's changing mores. Properly appreciating his writing thus requires less emphasis on how "circumstances" interfered with his art and more on how they compelled it.

Childhood and literary apprenticeship (1896–1917)

As with many writers, the first circumstance that Fitzgerald had to overcome was his immediate family. As the *New Yorker* politely put it in 1926, "His success was a great surprise to the home circle ... [for] the Fitzgeralds were not what is known as literary people."[4] Although Fitzgerald claimed that his father co-authored an unpublished novel, Edward Fitzgerald (1853–1931) served him mainly as a symbol of failure. When his only son was born on September 24, 1896, the genteel furniture manufacturer presided over an unprofitable wicker works in St Paul, Minnesota. The firm's closing two years later, coupled with Edward's subsequent undistinguished career as a wholesale grocery salesman, led Fitzgerald to dismiss his father alternately as a "moron" and, more generously, as representative of that "good heart that came from another America" – that is, the Victorian age that modernity had rendered obsolete.[5] The defining event of Fitzgerald's childhood was Edward's 1908 firing from Procter and Gamble, for whom the family had relocated to Buffalo and Syracuse, New York, during his infancy. Memories of that humiliation would resurface whenever the son doubted his own merits. "He had lost his essential drive, his immaculateness of purpose," Fitzgerald reflected. "He was a failure the rest of his days" (*In His Own Time* 297). Defeatism was not merely a personal flaw; it was indicative of his father's "tired old stock," which had "very little left of vitality and mental energy" (*Apprentice Fiction* 178). Edward's matrilineal lineage could be traced to a founding pair of Maryland families, the Scotts and the Keys, which included Fitzgerald's namesake, Francis Scott Key, author of "The Star-Spangled Banner." Yet the Civil War superannuated the legacy of Southern nobility in which Edward was reared, leading Fitzgerald to ascribe his mediocrity to historical upheaval. "I wonder how deep the Civil War was in [him]," he wrote in 1940, recalling tales of Edward's childhood days ferrying Confederate spies across the Potomac. "What a sense of honor and duty ... How lost [his generation] seemed in the changing world ... struggling to keep their children in the *haute bourgeoisie* when their like were sinking into obscur[ity]."[6]

Quite oppositely, Fitzgerald's mother, Mary or "Mollie" (1860–1936), represented the gaucheries of the upper-middle-class parvenu. The daughter of Irish immigrant Philip F. McQuillan (1834–1877), who between 1859 and his death built a modest general store into a million-dollar wholesale grocery business, she was a monied but peripheral figure in her native St Paul. Known for her eccentric habits and disheveled demeanor, she was considered by her son a "funny old wraith" (*Letters* 418) and "a neurotic, half insane with pathological worry."[7] Her neuroses were not unreasonable; three months before Fitzgerald was born, his parents lost two daughters, Mary and Louise, and another would die in infancy in 1900. Fear over her children's safety – the only other surviving sibling, Annabel, was born in 1901 – caused Mollie to spoil them, a habit that Fitzgerald blamed for his vanity and narcissism. ("I didn't know till 15 there was anyone in the world except me," he confessed [*Letters* 419]). His mixed feelings for Mollie are obvious in the treatment of Beatrice Blaine in *This Side of Paradise* (1920); thanks to her dithering pampering, Beatrice's protagonist son, Amory, is imbued with an "aristocratic egotism" of which the plot goes to great lengths to divest him.[8] At least some of Fitzgerald's resentment reflected his defensiveness for his father, for he grew up hearing his mother wonder aloud how the family would survive without McQuillan money, their main source of support after their 1908 return to St Paul. Later in life, it arose from Scott's own dependency. In a sad echo of Edward, he had to rely upon loans from Mollie in the mid-1930s to finesse his debts.

Fitzgerald's second immediate childhood influence was St Paul itself, a predominantly Catholic, affluent city whose "topography of bluffs and flats (the rich perched on a rim above, the working class on the plain below), no doubt encouraged Fitzgerald's fierce awareness of social and class distinctions."[9] The distinctions were also geographic: after 1908, the Fitzgeralds rented a series of apartments and homes along the outer edges of Summit Avenue, St Paul's residential showcase. Although a playmate of wealthy scions, Scott was keenly aware that he was not a member of the *haut monde*. As a result, he suffered a lifelong inferiority complex that, consciously or not, he exacerbated by striking relationships with wealthy cliques. André LeVot claims that the resulting resentment led Fitzgerald to depict the self-styled "Boston of the Middle West" as a land of "coupon clippers straining toward worldliness and the Victorian virtues."[10] The characterization overstates the case, yet it does convey the disdain Fitzgerald felt for the provincial insularity and self-congratulatory humility of an elite whose prosperity arose from such unglamorous mercantile endeavors as dry goods and shipping. (St Paul's most influential citizen was railroad magnate James J. Hill, whose name often surfaces in his work.)

Although St Paul was not a literary environment, Scott displayed an early aptitude for writing. Yet he was an indifferent student both at the private St Paul Academy (1908–11) and later at the Newman School (1911–13), the Catholic boarding facility in Hackensack, New Jersey, where his parents sent him in hopes of disciplining his studies. Biographers frequently credit his poor academic performance to his self-absorption. As Arthur Mizener puts it, he was "incapable of learning anything that did not appeal to his imagination."[11] His classroom failures have resulted in the major misconception that he was, in the words of Glenway Wescott, "the worst educated man in the world."[12] In fact, Fitzgerald read widely, especially in modern literature and history.

Contemporaries like Wescott (1901–1987) and Edmund Wilson (1895–1972), the future "dean of American critics" with whom Fitzgerald became friends when he entered Princeton University in 1913, doubted his intellectual depth. Yet his style of learning was a departure, not a delinquency, from their more erudite ways. His thought process was experiential, meaning he grasped knowledge through effusion instead of ratiocination. Although Fitzgerald cited Wilson as his "intellectual conscience" (*Crack-Up* 178), his most simpatico mentor was actually Father Sigourney Webster Fay (1875–1919), the Catholic priest and Newman trustee whom he met in 1912. *This Side of Paradise* suggests the fanciful flavor of their philosophical exchanges: "[Their dialogue] saw Amory's mind turned inside out, a hundred of his theories confirmed, and his joy of life crystallized to a thousand ambitions. Not that the conversation was scholastic – heaven forbid! . . . Monsignor . . . [took] good care that Amory never once felt out of his depth" (32). "Scholastic" peers made Fitzgerald feel "out of his depth" because they considered his emotional identification with ideas capricious and solipsistic; Fay taught him to experience knowledge as "a dazzling, golden thing," "dispelling its oppressive mugginess" and divesting it of "plaintive ritual" so it exuded the "romantic glamour" that was the key motivator of his imagination (*In His Own Time* 134).

Despite Fitzgerald's disinterest in formal education, his schooling shaped his sensibility in important ways. Most obviously, high school and college reinforced his sense of social hierarchy, for their student bodies were segregated by a strict adolescent caste system that regulated opportunities for distinction. Although Fitzgerald wrote for school publications, including eight early stories featured in Princeton's *Nassau Literary Magazine*, his dreams of football heroism proved unrealizable, and poor grades prevented him from pursuing extracurricular renown. In 1915 a failed makeup examination in quantitative analysis rendered him ineligible for the presidency of Princeton's student theater company, the Triangle Club, for which he had already written the lyrics for two well-received productions, *Fie! Fie! Fi-Fi!* and *The Evil Eye*. Fitzgerald would go to his grave believing that this failure marked the moment "my career as a leader of men was over," for not attaining a prominent social position undermined his already tenuous sense of Ivy League legitimacy (*Crack-Up* 76). ("We're the damned middle-class," *This Side of Paradise*'s Amory laments when his ambitions are foiled [49].) Although his preening efforts to compensate for his uncertain status earned Fitzgerald derision – at Newman he was considered "fresh," while at Princeton he had a reputation for "running it out" (i.e., talking about himself) – undergraduate competition imbued him with two dichotomous traits: while he coveted qualities in other men that he felt he lacked, he also cast himself to the forefront of his cohort by imagining himself ideally suited for defining its character.

The first tendency again manifests his perpetual self-doubt, for Fitzgerald constantly deferred to more self-assured role models like Wilson. "When I like men I want to be like them," he admitted. "I don't want the man. I want to absorb into myself all the qualities that make him attractive and leave him out."[13] The second trait compensates for that insecurity by deeming his failures endemic of his peers' precarious place in the adult world. While acknowledging that "everything bad" at Princeton "was my own fault" (*Ledger* 170), Fitzgerald also blamed his scholastic deficiencies on Princeton's pedantic faculty, who had "an uncanny knack for making literature distasteful to young men" (*Afternoon of an Author* 75). By ascribing a personal fault to generational conflict, he could attribute his disappointments to external obstacles that, in turn, represented barriers faced by all youth his age – a major reason why he would soon be singled out as their spokesman.

Accompanying his collegiate letdowns were romantic travails that proved equally essential to his sensibility. In January 1915 Fitzgerald met Ginevra King, a banker's daughter from Lake Forest, Illinois, whose reputation for coquetry was well known in St Paul. To an ardent though sexually conservative suitor – one for whom the pursuit of romance was more intriguing than its conquest – Ginevra was as much a symbol as a person: attractive, haughty from privilege, and mildly rebellious (her father withdrew her from Westover in 1916 after she was caught talking to boys from her dormitory window), she embodied the glamorous life that Fitzgerald coveted. She also excited his insecurities over whether he was worthy of it. As Ginevra's recently rediscovered diary and correspondence reveal, "She knew that he was idealizing her and urged him . . . not to do so, but of course he did. Ginevra was pleased by Scott's attention, but she was put off by his attempts to analyze her personality and by his persistent jealousy."[14] Their inevitable breakup proved even more grievous than Edward's firing or his Princeton failures. Visiting Ginevra's family in August 1916, Fitzgerald overheard someone (accounts vary as to who) remark, "Poor boys shouldn't think of marrying rich girls" (*Ledger* 17). It was The Snub that Launched a Career, for it became the defining motif of his fiction. Without identifying Ginevra by name, Fitzgerald publicly admitted in 1935 that his heroines were based on "my first girl 18–20 whom I've used over and over and never forgotten" (*In His Own Time* 177).

Zelda and early success (1918–1924)

By mid-1917, Fitzgerald had few other options for consoling his misfortunes than to join the Army. America's April 6 entry into World War I had inspired a wave of national pride, but Fitzgerald disassociated himself from the "wine-bibbers of patriotism" by describing his likely death as a fulfillment of the romantic destiny that Princeton had denied him: "I may get killed for America – but I'm going to die for myself," he boasted (*Letters* 414). Commissioned as a second lieutenant on October 26, he reported to Fort Leavenworth, Kansas, where, convinced that he "had only three months to live" because "in those days all infantry officers thought they had only three months to live" (*Afternoon of an Author* 84), he dashed off a 120,000-word potpourri of narrative and verse entitled "The Romantic Egotist." Reassignments in the spring of 1918 sent him to Louisville, Kentucky, to Augusta, Georgia, and, finally, to Montgomery, Alabama, where as a member of the 67th Infantry Regiment at Camp Sheridan he submitted his manuscript to the prestigious publisher Charles Scribner's Sons. While awaiting a reply, he attended country-club dances, including a fateful one in July where he met Zelda Sayre, the daughter of the chief justice of the Alabama State Supreme Court. Although barely two months out of high school and not yet eighteen, Zelda basked in her reputation as Montgomery's preeminent belle, "convinced," she would remember, "that the only thing of any significance was to take what she wanted when she could."[15] As Ruth Prigozy notes, Zelda "was the perfect girl for young Scott: beautiful, independent, brilliant in conversation, and correspondence, socially prominent (although not wealthy), and as eager as he was for success – although in her case, the goal was amorphous." As with Ginevra, there was an additional element of allure: "Fitzgerald was not only attracted to her considerable charms, but also to her status as the most popular girl."[16]

Their courtship was not immediately serious – he cited September 7 as the day he officially fell in love (*Ledger* 173) – but it was full of adolescent passion and intrigue. Zelda taunted Scott with her bevy of suitors, which included several other Camp Sheridan officers. As he would recall in "The Last of the Belles" (1929), her regional charms were irresistible:

> There she was – the Southern type in all its purity . . . She had the
> adroitness sugar-coated with sweet, voluble simplicity, the suggested
> background of devoted fathers, brothers and admirers stretching back
> into the South's heroic age, the unfailing coolness acquired in the
> endless struggle with the heat. There were notes in her voice that order
> slaves around, that withered up Yankee captains, and then soft,
> wheedling notes that mingled in unfamiliar loveliness with the night.[17]

Despite their grandiloquent romance, Zelda was wary of marrying a man whose military pay totaled $141 a month. Their on-again off-again relationship, which included a broken engagement, was but one frustration Fitzgerald suffered in 1918–19. Although Scribner's lauded "The Romantic Egotist," the book was rejected because of its unruly form and inconclusive ending. As his regiment was preparing to embark for Europe from Camp Mills, Long Island, that November, the Armistice abruptly ended his "haughty career as the army's worst aide-de-camp" (*Crack-Up* 85). Upon his discharge the following February, he accepted a lowly copywriter's position at the advertising agency Barron, Collier. Although he completed nineteen stories that spring, he claimed that he had 122 rejections. Convinced that he would never win Zelda back unless he became a successful novelist, he repaired to his parents' home to frantically recast "Egotist" into *This Side of Paradise*:

> I was in love with a whirlwind, and I must spin a net big enough to catch it out of my head, a head full of trickling nickels and sliding dimes, the incessant music box of the poor. It couldn't be done like that, so when the girl threw me over I went home and finished my novel. And then, suddenly, everything changed.   (*Crack-Up* 86)

Thanks to the enthusiasm of editor Maxwell Perkins (1884–1947), Scribner's accepted the revision on September 16. Periodicals began buying his stories as well. In October *The Smart Set*, edited by tastemakers H. L. Mencken (1880–1956) and George Jean Nathan (1882–1958), paid $215 for six contributions, while *Scribner's Magazine* offered $300 for two pieces. The real breakthrough came when Fitzgerald's recently acquired agent, Harold Ober (1881–1959), sold "Head and Shoulders" for $360 to the *Saturday Evening Post*, whose readership topped two million. All told, Fitzgerald sold twenty stories in 1919–20, his total income leaping from a modest $879 to an impressive $18,175, including $7,425 alone from movie options to three stories.[18]

Flushed with success, Scott married Zelda in the vestry of St Patrick's Cathedral in New York on April 3, 1920, two weeks after the publication of *This Side of Paradise*. Although sales exceeded Scribner's expectations, the novel's influence far outstripped its profits. Fitzgerald capitalized on his sudden notoriety by serving as an expert on teenage mores, offering audacious insights into his generation's propensity for "petting" (i.e., kissing), drinking (which the recent advent of Prohibition had done little to curtail), and unapologetic materialism. *Paradise*'s immediate legacy, however, was to popularize the term *flapper*. At Fitzgerald's request Scribner's promoted it as "A Novel About Flappers Written for Philosophers." The alliteration was so irresistible that, despite concerns over its faddishness, in September he titled his first story collection *Flappers and Philosophers*. And while Zelda was more properly a belle than a flapper, she obligingly bobbed her hair, adopted prevailing New York fashions, and played the role of muse in celebrity interviews and profiles.

The popular image of the Fitzgeralds as cosmopolitan carousers arises from the raucous yet relatively brief New York honeymoon in April 1920, a period whose escapades have become legendary: "They rode down Fifth Avenue on the tops of taxis because it was hot or dove into the fountain at Union Square or tried to undress at the [Broadway play] *Scandals*, or, in sheer delight at the splendor of New York, jumped dead sober, into the Pulitzer fountain in front of the Plaza" (*Far Side* 140). Such behavior was inimical to writing, however, so in May the couple relocated to Westport, Connecticut. As Fitzgerald struggled to follow up *Paradise*, friends unfairly blamed Zelda for distracting him: "If she's [home] Fitz can't work – she bothers him," Princeton acquaintance Alexander McKaig wrote in his diary, an oft-cited source for this heady period. "If she's not there he can't work – worried what she might do."[19]

The problem actually lay in Fitzgerald's conflicting visions of literature as a lifestyle and as a profession. While the former promised privileged, reckless indulgence, the latter required discipline, which is why, as Matthew J. Bruccoli notes, "He was a methodical planner all his professional life, preparing schedules and charts for his work; that he rarely kept to these plans did not discourage him from making them" (*Epic Grandeur* 168). Because Fitzgerald's fiction was autobiographical, he also needed constant if not melodramatic stimulation, for without that inspiration, he had nothing to write about. The point is corroborated by the plot he settled on for his next book: "My new novel concerns the life of Anthony Patch . . . how he and his beautiful young wife are wrecked upon the shoals of dissipation" (*A Life in Letters* 41).

Fitzgerald completed an unsatisfactory draft of *The Beautiful and Damned* in April 1921. Although serial rights netted $7,000, such windfalls did little to discourage his and Zelda's profligacy, and he was forced to borrow from both Scribner's and Ober, a habit that would continue until his death. After an unpleasant European sojourn, the couple settled in St Paul to await the October 26 birth of their only child, Frances or "Scottie" (1921–1986). While revising his novel, Fitzgerald completed "The Diamond as Big as the Ritz" (1922), a fantastical satire of American materialism that proved too cutting for the *Saturday Evening Post*, which preferred flapper romances. While a story like "The Popular Girl" (1922) could earn $1,500, "Diamond" garnered a comparatively paltry $300 from *The Smart Set*, wrenching ever wider the gap between Fitzgerald's commercial and literary prospects.

When *The Beautiful and Damned* appeared in March 1922, reviewers acknowledged Fitzgerald's stylistic facility but dismissed his ambition to write serious literature. Even friends doubted his capacity for weighty inquiry: "His ideas are too often treated like paper crackers," fellow Princetonian John Peale Bishop (1892–1944) decided. "Things to make a gay and pretty noise with and then be cast aside."[20] Unfortunately, Fitzgerald encouraged this perception by deprecating his work. When his second story collection, *Tales of the Jazz Age*, appeared in September 1922, he annotated its table of contents with mocking commentary, boasting of writing "The Camel's Back" (1920) in eleven hours and claiming that, despite the kudos received for "Diamond," he preferred "The Offshore Pirate" (1920). His blasé attitude toward a minor effort, "Jemina" (1916; revised 1921), even predicted the ebb of his popularity: "It seems to me worth preserving for a few years – at least until the ennui of changing fashions suppresses me, my books, and it together."[21]

Although *The Beautiful and Damned* and *Tales of the Jazz Age* were successful, selling upwards of 50,000 and 24,000 copies respectively, Fitzgerald continued to covet extra-literary earning opportunities. Hoping that Broadway might provide a steady income stream, he wrote a three-act farce called *The Vegetable*, a satire about a lowly mailman elected president that required six revisions before interesting a producer. His screenwriting career was no more successful. Although he earned $13,500 from the film industry in 1923, the majority was for movie rights, not for the scripts and scenarios he submitted to studios. Fitzgerald squandered nearly two years pursuing these opportunities, even moving in late 1922 to New York City's ritziest suburb, Great Neck on Long Island, to mingle with theater and movie impresarios.

The stories he did manage to complete were important, however, for they found him rehearsing themes and plots for what would become his third novel. Known nowadays as the "*Gatsby* cluster," these include one certified classic ("Winter Dreams", 1922) and such estimable efforts as "Absolution" and "'The Sensible Thing'" (both 1924). As Bruccoli writes, "These stories variously deal with the aspiration for and the corruption of wealth, the love of a poor boy for an unattainable girl, and the connection between love and money."[22] Little progress could be made on the novel until a disastrous Atlantic City staging of *The Vegetable* in November 1923 convinced Fitzgerald that the stage was not his forte. "People rustled their programs and talked audibly in bored impatient whispers," he recalled. "After the second act I wanted to stop the show and say it was all a mistake" (*Afternoon of an Author* 93–4).

During the winter of 1923–4, he churned out nearly a dozen *Saturday Evening Post* stories, earning $16,450 to finance his novel. To economize, he and Zelda relocated to the French Riviera, whose favorable exchange rate of nineteen francs to the dollar made their lifestyle more affordable. There they made friends with Gerald and Sara Murphy (1888–1964 and 1883–1975, respectively), a wealthy couple whose Cap d'Antibes home, the Villa America, was the epicenter of expatriate glamor. That July, the Fitzgeralds' marriage suffered a serious blow when Zelda became involved with a French aviator, Edouard Jozan. Although biographers disagree over whether the affair was consummated, Fitzgerald nevertheless felt betrayed, believing that "something had happened that could never be repaired" (*Notebooks* 113). Inevitably, his anguish colors *The Great Gatsby*. When Daisy Buchanan confesses that she loves both Gatsby and her husband, Tom, one senses Fitzgerald's shock at discovering that the romance he believed so singular was compromised. The crisis lent pathos to his writing. Upon receiving the manuscript that November, Perkins recognized the artistic leap it represented: "The amount of meaning you get into a sentence, the dimensions and intensity of the impressions you make a paragraph carry, are most extraordinary . . . You once told me you were not a *natural* writer – my God! You have plainly mastered the craft, of course; but you needed far more than craftsmanship for this."[23]

Artistic maturity and personal decline (1925–1934)

Literati from T. S. Eliot (1888–1965) to Gertrude Stein (1874–1946) also praised *The Great Gatsby*, yet sales stalled at 23,000 copies. Two weeks after its April 10, 1925, publication, Fitzgerald was in Paris, where he met Ernest Hemingway (1899–1961). The previous fall, Scott had admired either one or both of Hemingway's first privately printed collections, *Three Stories and Ten Poems* (1923) and *in our time* (1924), and had recommended him to Perkins. Their friendship now established, he set about advancing Hemingway's career through book reviews and correspondence, finessing his entry into the Scribner's fold, and even offering editorial advice on Hemingway's debut novel, *The Sun Also Rises* (1926). Hemingway would repay these favors by portraying Fitzgerald as a henpecked drunkard in his posthumous memoir, *A Moveable Feast* (1964), notoriously claiming that Fitzgerald asked him to assess his penis size because "Zelda said the way I was built I could never make any woman happy."[24] Hemingway's disdain for Zelda was mutual; she denounced him as "phony as a rubber check."[25] Although her husband saw Hemingway only intermittently after 1926, their relationship proved a major source of contention between the couple, with Scott even claiming that Zelda accused the men of being "fairies."[26]

After *The Great Gatsby*, Fitzgerald planned a fourth novel variously titled "The World's Fair," "The Boy Who Killed His Mother," and "Our Type." Little was accomplished, however, because Scott and Zelda were drinking heavily. Over the next four years, only four chapters or 20,000 words were completed. (They appear in recast form in *Tender Is the Night*, 1934.) His short-story career also suffered. Although his third collection, *All the Sad Young Men*, was warmly reviewed in February 1926 – it includes several important works, including "The Rich Boy" (1926) – he was unable to complete another story until June 1927. The unhealthiness of expatriate life is suggested by a contemporaneous *New Yorker* profile. In 1922 Fitzgerald had objected when Edmund Wilson referenced his drinking in a *Bookman* review, but now he was introducing himself to journalists with a dipsomaniacal motto: "Don't you know I am one of the most notorious drinkers of the younger generation?" (*In His Own Time* 443).

Hoping for a more settled environment, the Fitzgeralds returned to America in December 1926. Deep in debt, Scott accepted a $3,500 advance to write a flapper comedy entitled *Lipstick*, but Hollywood rejected his perfunctory script. His marriage suffered further strain when he became infatuated with seventeen-year-old starlet Lois Moran (1909–1990), the inspiration for *Tender Is the Night*'s Rosemary Hoyt. Although their relationship was probably chaste, it made his marriage as fractious as had Zelda's infatuation with Jozan, with Zelda burning her clothes in the bathtub of the Ambassador Hotel and later destroying a platinum wristwatch that Scott had given her in 1920.

By 1927, Zelda was seeking an outlet for her own creativity. That March, the couple rented a Wilmington, Delaware, estate known as Ellerslie, where for a period of "judicious tranquility," she painted, wrote stories for *College Humor*, and studied ballet with the Philadelphia Opera (*Crack-Up* 47). The Fitzgeralds even returned to Paris in April 1928 so that Zelda could work with Lubov Egorova of the Ballets Russes. Despite the optimistic progress reports to Perkins, work on Scott's novel had ground to a halt. Yet this period was hardly unproductive, for he did complete nine semi-autobiographical stories tracing the maturation of Basil Duke Lee from ages ten to seventeen. Although these efforts netted $31,500, Fitzgerald "was a little embarrassed by the Basil series; not by the stories themselves, most of which were excellent, but by the circumstance that he was writing stories about adolescents for the *Post*" (*Epic Grandeur* 311). Over the next several years, as he produced five additional entries featuring Basil's female opposite, the Ginevra-esque debutante Josephine Perry, Fitzgerald would decline invitations to republish his "juveniles" as a stopgap volume. His ambivalence toward such enviable work suggests how deeply his financial dependency on the *Saturday Evening Post* prejudiced him against short fiction. Indeed, by the spring of 1929, as his price per story peaked at $4,000, Fitzgerald denounced himself as a prostitute paid extravagantly "because she's mastered the 40 positions – in her youth one was enough" (*A Life in Letters* 169). Significantly, this self-denigration appears in a letter to Hemingway, whose reputation as a literary purist was approaching its acme. By this point, Hemingway had little use for his friend. When Fitzgerald offered perceptive criticism on *A Farewell to Arms* (1929), its irate author scribbled "Kiss My Ass" on the manuscript (*Hemingway vs. Fitzgerald* 126).

Meanwhile, Zelda's dance regime strained the Fitzgeralds' marriage and depleted her reserves. Invited to join the San Carlo Opera Ballet Company in Naples in September 1929, she was unable to break her dependency on Scott and spiraled into hallucinatory episodes that culminated in her April 23, 1930, entry into the Paris-based Malmaison clinic. By summer, she had been hospitalized twice more, first in the Valmont Clinic in Glion, Switzerland, and then in the Prangins Clinic in nearby Nyon, where she remained under the care of Dr Oscar Forel until September 1931. Much debate remains about the precise nature of Zelda's mental illness. Admission reports cite her obsessive work habits and her "fear of becoming a homosexual" because "she thinks she is in love with her dance teacher" (qtd. in *Epic Grandeur* 343). While the Sayre family blamed Scott's alcoholism, he attributed it to their long history of mental instability, including the suicides of both Zelda's maternal grandmother and aunt.[27] Dr Forel diagnosed schizophrenia and instituted a "reeducation program" involving tranquilizers, physical restraint, and hypnosis. Fitzgerald's explanation was more symbolic: just as the October 1929 stockmarket crash seemed inevitable retribution for the Jazz Age's lack of accounting, so, too, Zelda's breakdown was payback for their years of irresponsibility. He noted the parallel in his *Ledger* – "*The Crash! Zelda + America*" – and explored it in his writing (184). His most-anthologized story, "Babylon Revisited," and essay, "Echoes of the Jazz Age" (both 1931), resonate with remorse for the wastage of the boom years.

Upon Zelda's release from Prangins, the Fitzgeralds briefly returned to Montgomery before Scott accepted a \$1,200-a-week offer from Metro-Goldwyn-Mayer to script the Jean Harlow vehicle *Red-Headed Woman*. His second attempt at screenwriting was also unsuccessful; the novelist Anita Loos, whose *Gentlemen Prefer Blondes* (1925) exploited the flapper vogue he had inaugurated, was hired to replace him. In February 1932, while vacationing in St Petersburg, Florida, Zelda suffered a relapse and was institutionalized at Johns Hopkins University's Phipps Clinic in Baltimore, Maryland. There she completed a thinly veiled account of her marriage entitled *Save Me the Waltz*, which she submitted to Scribner's without her husband's knowledge. Irate, Fitzgerald accused her of poaching his material. Although he eventually consented to *Waltz*'s publication (it was neither a critical nor commercial success, selling just 1,400 copies and earning a paltry \$120 in royalties), the charge raised serious questions about the literary property rights to their lives. As Zelda's biographers have been quick to note, Scott showed little compunction about borrowing from her letters and diaries in his early work and publishing her essays and stories under a joint byline when doing so could command a higher price. Tensions boiled over during a May 28, 1933, conference with Zelda's psychiatrist at La Paix, the Victorian estate that Fitzgerald rented in Baltimore. As Scott condemned Zelda as a "third-rate" talent, she demanded a divorce. As always, they recognized their reputation as public performers:

> *Zelda.* What is our marriage, anyway? It has been nothing but a long battle ever since I can remember.
> *Fitzgerald.* I don't know about that. We were about the most envied couple in about 1921 in America.
> *Zelda.* I guess so. We were awfully good showmen.
>
> (qtd. in *Epic Grandeur* 414)

Arguably, Fitzgerald needed the competitive shock of Zelda's literary ambitions to complete his novel. By August 1932, he decided it would examine "the break up of a fine personality . . . caused not by flabbiness but really tragic forces such as the inner conflicts of the idealist and the compromises forced upon him by circumstances." Naturally, those circumstances would include the mental illness of protagonist Dick Diver's wife, Nicole, whose medical history closely parallels Zelda's. Fitzgerald also planned to comment on the broader conditions of modernity – the unreality of modern life, the moral aimlessness of expatriation, the tumult of postwar European politics, all of which would make the book "a novel of our time."[28] Fitzgerald completed it in October 1933, whereupon it was serialized in *Scribner's Magazine* after a last-minute title change from *Doctor Diver's Holiday* (originally *The Drunkard's Holiday*) to *Tender Is the Night*, a phrase borrowed from his favorite Romantic poet, John Keats (1795–1821).

With nine years of personal and professional frustrations invested in *Tender Is the Night*, it was inevitable that anything short of a rapturous reception would feel like a failure. Although the book sold some 12,000 copies and briefly made *Publishers Weekly*'s bestseller list, reviews were ambivalent. Critics acknowledged the elegiac style but criticized the structure as diffuse – an opinion that Fitzgerald came to share. "I would give anything if I hadn't had to write Part III of *Tender Is the Night* entirely on stimulant," he told Perkins in 1935. "If I had one more crack at it cold sober I believe it might have made a great difference" (*Dear Scott/Dear Max* 219).

The crack-up and the comeback (1935–1940)

The irony of *Tender Is the Night* is that Nicole's rehabilitation comes at the cost of her husband's vitality. Yet even before the book's April 12, 1934, publication,

Zelda suffered a relapse that necessitated her return to Phipps. As Fitzgerald struggled to pay for her treatment, she transferred to Craig House in Beacon, New York, and then to the Sheppard and Enoch Pratt Hospital back in Baltimore. By 1933, his earnings had dwindled to $12,000 (*Epic Grandeur* 642). Although *Taps at Reveille* (1935), a short-story collection and his last book published during his lifetime, addressed an unusually broad range of topics – "The Night Before Chancellorsville" (1935) is a Civil War tale, while "Family in the Wind" (1932) involves a tornado disaster – commercial fiction was now beyond his abilities. Columnist O. O. McIntyre suggested that Fitzgerald's early success had pigeonholed him:

> F. Scott Fitzgerald, graying and chunking up, is reputedly one of the most difficult authors from whom editors may wrangle a story these days. He is the literary symbol of an era – the era of the new generation – and editors continue to want stories of flask gin and courteous collegiates preceding ladies through windshields on midnight joy rides. The public has acquired this Fitzgerald taste, too. But Fitzgerald has taken an elderly and serious turn. Mellowed is the term. He wants to write mellowly, too. And if they won't let him he won't write at all. So there.[29]

In reality, Fitzgerald was stymied by alcohol. When drunk, he would telephone magazine editors, haranguing them to accept his stories. Eager for any niche, he turned to the new men's magazine *Esquire*, which promised $250 per article, an 80 percent drop from his peak-selling price. The compensation was artistic freedom; encouraged by editor Arnold Gingrich (1903–1976), Fitzgerald began to explore his misfortunes in confessional non-fiction that unsettlingly combined nostalgia and self-recrimination.

Early entries such as "Sleeping and Waking" and the Zelda-penned "Show Mr. and Mrs. F. to Number – " (both 1934) garnered little attention, but the culminating triptych, collectively known as *The Crack-Up*, incited controversy in 1936. Although hardly candid by today's standards, the essays are lyrically compelling and yet transparently evasive; no mention is made of Zelda's illness, and alcohol is addressed only to deny its negative effect. Most damagingly, their defeated aura seemed to substantiate Fitzgerald's reputation as a has-been. In response, Hemingway ungenerously described Scott as "wrecked" in "The Snows of Kilimanjaro" (1936) (also published in *Esquire*). Yet the most devastating fallout occurred when *New York Post* reporter Michel Mok interviewed an intoxicated Fitzgerald on his fortieth birthday. As the *Post*'s apt headline announced, the author now resided "on the other side of paradise . . . engulfed in despair" (*In His Own Time* 294–9). The portrait was so injurious that Fitzgerald claimed he attempted suicide.

By mid-1937, Fitzgerald's debts topped $22,000, and his earnings had dropped to $3,500, roughly half of the annual cost of Zelda's treatment at Highland Hospital in Asheville, North Carolina. Desperate, he turned once more to Hollywood for financial relief. Studios were reluctant to hire him, though he eventually secured a $1,000-a-week contract from MGM. His tenure proved profitable – $85,000 over eighteen months – though not prolific: his only screen credit was for the war melodrama *Three Comrades* (1938). In January 1939 MGM declined to renew his option, forcing him to scramble for freelance opportunities. When United Artists hired him to co-write the collegiate romance *Winter Carnival* that February, he went on such a bender during a research trip to Dartmouth College that he and collaborator Budd Schulberg were fired.

By this point, the Fitzgeralds were married only in name. The couple regularly corresponded, yet Scott and Zelda saw each other only three times after 1937, mainly because Scott (unbeknown to Zelda) was involved with Hollywood gossip columnist Sheilah Graham (1904–1988). While Zelda's health precluded much of a maternal relationship with Scottie, Fitzgerald became an active parent, lecturing his daughter on adolescent proprieties and compiling reading lists to supplement her Vassar education. (He devised a similar curriculum for Sheilah.) This period also marks his most serious attempts at sobriety. He did not drink during his first few months at MGM. After October 1937, his affair with Graham was disrupted by occasional yet violent alcoholic episodes recounted in her memoirs.[30]

Fitzgerald returned to fiction after his MGM contract expired, but his stories were now unsaleable. In July 1939 he broke with Harold Ober when his agent refused to advance him money against future work. Despite these setbacks, he began to outline a new novel, a *roman à clef* about wunderkind producer Irving Thalberg (1899–1936), whom Fitzgerald had met in 1927. "Unlike *Tender Is the Night* it is not the story of deterioration," he reported to *Collier's* editor Kenneth Littauer. "It is not depressing and not morbid in spite of the tragic ending. If one book could ever be 'like' another I should say it is more 'like' *The Great Gatsby* than any other of my books. But I hope it will be entirely different – I hope it will be something new" (*A Life in Letters* 412). Fitzgerald hoped to finance the novel's completion with a serialization deal with *Collier's*, but after reviewing the opening chapter, Littauer declined his $15,000 asking price. Once again, the author turned to *Esquire*, which accepted a series of seventeen satirical Hollywood stories about Pat Hobby, a down-on-his-luck studio flack.

Fitzgerald labored over his novel between August 1939 and December 1940. Although he generated some 1,100 pages of manuscript – as well as 200 of background notes – his health was in rapid decline. In November 1940 he suffered a cardiac spasm while shopping at Hollywood's famous Schwab's Drugstore. Ordered to avoid exerting himself, he spent the next several weeks in bed, using a board for a desk. Less than a month later, another spasm occurred as he and Sheilah attended a movie premiere. The following day, Saturday, December 21, while awaiting a house call from his doctor, he suffered a third attack that proved fatal. In one of his last letters to Zelda, he had assured her he would recuperate: "The cardiogram shows that my heart is repairing itself but it will be a gradual process that will take some months. It is odd that the heart is one of the organs that does repair itself."[31]

Fitzgerald's last royalty check from Scribner's, dated a few months before his death, totaled $13.13. Although obituaries and the posthumous publication of *The Last Tycoon* in 1941 inspired a spate of career assessments, it would take most of the 1940s to elevate his literary stature. In the meantime, Zelda, who had returned to Montgomery in May 1940 to live with her mother, continued to paint, write, and occasionally share stories about her life with Scott with curious college students. During unstable periods, she returned to Highland Hospital, where on March 10, 1948, she and several other patients died from smoke inhalation during a fire in the sanitarium's main wing. The tragedy of her death at the relatively young age of forty-seven – Scott himself was only forty-four – calls to mind a line from one of Scott's final letters, which also serves as an apt epitaph for their lives: "Cards began falling badly for us much too early" (*A Life in Letters* 452).

Chapter 2

Cultural context

With the exception of the 1960s, no decade inspires as much fascination as the 1920s. After nearly a century, its representative figures – whether Charlie Chaplin (1889–1977), Charles Lindbergh (1902–1974), or, of course, F. Scott Fitzgerald – remain American icons, while both the era's high art and its passing fads still serve as defining cultural reference points. Clothing lines and home decor collections evoke period fashions and design trends, and repercussions from the broader phenomena responsible for making the time so tumultuous (the expansion and proliferation of mass media, consumerism, sexual liberation) continue to be felt today. Unlike, say, the 1950s – which did not arouse much interest until the mid-1970s when a wave of post-Watergate retrospection prompted a pining for its (supposed) calm and simplicity – nostalgia for the Jazz Age was immediate. The decade had barely ended when Frederick Lewis Allen published his popular *Only Yesterday: An Informal History of the 1920s*, which catalogued a vibrant confluence of trends and milestones suddenly rendered remote by the Great Depression. That same year, Fitzgerald published his own assessment of the era, "Echoes of the Jazz Age" (1931), which more mournfully recalls it as "an age of excess" during which "a whole race [turned] hedonistic, deciding on pleasure."[1] As this quotation suggests, the 1920s are remembered as a time of innocent indulgence when prosperity appeared limitless, impulses bore no consequence, and irresponsibility was a birthright. As always, the reality was more complex. The period was actually a whirlwind of transformation during which everyday life struggled to accommodate the flux of modern times.

My generation: youth culture and the politics of aging

A fundamental influence on Fitzgerald was the century's shifting attitudes toward youth. One need not venture far into his fiction to recognize how age was his chief index of integrity, with the vitality and enthusiasm of his teenage and post-adolescent protagonists opposing their elders' stodgy conservatism. *This Side of Paradise* (1920), "Winter Dreams" (1922), "Emotional Bankruptcy" (1931), and many others climax with characters' epiphanic realization that, as "The Last of the Belles" (1929) puts it, they are doomed to grow "doggy in [their] old age."[2] Other works editorialize on specific chronological milestones: "People over forty can seldom be permanently convinced of anything," reads a typical interjection in "Bernice Bobs Her Hair" (1920). "At eighteen our convictions are ills from which we look; at forty-five they are caves in which we hide" (*Short Stories* 31). Similarly, much of Fitzgerald's early fame arose from gossip-column reports of his youthful insouciance, as when the *New York Tribune*'s Burton Rascoe claimed in 1922 that he had interrupted an important business meeting to pluck six offensive gray hairs from the beard of *Scribner's Magazine* editor Robert Bridges.[3] Such stories, however apocryphal, quickly stereotyped the author as the "Juvenile Juvenal of the Jeunesse Jazz," as the *New York Morning Telegraph* alliteratively labeled him.

Accusations of juvenility blamed the messenger and ignored the underlying conditions that allowed youth to excite both concern and envy. Adolescent character types like the flapper never would have become notable subcultural personae had a wave of age stratification not granted teenagers a distinct social space. Whether in schools, extracurricular activities, or unsupervised hours, young people became increasingly segregated from adults, with peer rather than parental affiliations determining their dress, language, and behavior. The more values developed along age-based lines, the more demographically distinct adolescents became. One reason why Fitzgerald and his contemporaries were so fond of generational monikers ("The Younger Generation," "The Rising Generation," "The Lost Generation," etc.) was that they had grown up with this cohort mindset, which inclined them to believe that they shared a collective maturation history. When Fitzgerald cheekily proclaimed in 1920 that "an author ought to write for the youth of his own generation," he was taking that notion a step further by insisting that the artist's contemporaries are his ideal audience because they, more than critics or teachers, understand the significance of the coming-of-age experiences he depicts.[4] As late as "Early Success" (1937), he would continue to insist, not unjustifiably, that a generation gap had prevented reviewers from appreciating his pre-*Gatsby* work:

> A lot of people thought [*This Side of Paradise*] was a fake, and perhaps
> it was, and a lot of others thought it was a lie, which it was not. . . .
> [columnist] Heywood Broun, who was on my trail[,] . . . comment[ed]
> that I seemed to be a very self-satisfied young man . . . I invited him
> to lunch and in a kindly way told him that it was too bad he had let his
> life slide away without accomplishing anything. He had just turned
> thirty and it was about then that I wrote a line which certain people
> will not let me forget: "She was a faded but still lovely woman of
> twenty-seven." (*Crack-Up* 88)

As silly as it may sound, Fitzgerald's claim that twenty-seven and thirty were thresholds of old age has historical merit, for an emerging preoccupation with retaining one's youth was making milestones of such dates. Nineteenth-century Romantics may have insisted that the child was the father of the man, yet their advocacy did little to erode older people's cultural authority, or to challenge the Victorian conception of children as apprentice adults. In the modern age, however, fears about the mechanization of everyday life excited a widespread coveting of the spontaneity of youth. "In our day and civilization, the hot life of feeling is remote and decadent," complained psychologist G. Stanley Hall, whose landmark study *Adolescence* (1904) is credited with legitimating adolescent development as a field of academic study. "Culture represses, and intellect saps the root . . . The life of feeling has its prime in youth, and we are prematurely old and too often senile in heart."[5] The goal of maturation, Hall and other social scientists argued, was not to extinguish or even regulate these passions but to stoke their flames throughout the lifecycle. What detractors like Broun misinterpreted as the flagrant immaturity of Fitzgerald's characters instead reflects this cultural urge to transcend the "mental limitations" to retain youthful verve. Yet the concomitant habit of regarding a particular birthday as the definitive onset of hoariness is indicative of the reciprocal worry that fanning the "hot life of feeling" might *prematurely* age a person by exhausting his or her resources. As Arthur Mizener argues, this fear is inherent in Fitzgerald's theory of emotional bankruptcy, in which the "extravagant expenditure" of "emotional capital" depletes youthful intensity, leaving protagonists like Tom Squires in "At Your Age" (1929) feeling "used up a little" (*Short Stories* 494).[6] Because senescence provided a conveniently inexorable biological process for dramatizing fears of diminishing vitality, the 1920s associated maturation with decline and fretted over what experiences could render one "old."

The theater of being: personality and performative identity

Another influential cultural trend was the new theatricality of daily life. Broun alluded to this phenomenon while chastising Fitzgerald for self-absorption: "The self-consciousness of Fitzgerald is a barrier which we are never able to pierce. He sees himself constantly not as a human being, but as a man in a novel or in a play. Every move is a picture and there is a camera man behind each tree" (qtd. in *Far Side* 128). Identity in the 1920s assumed an unprecedented performative dimension, with the traits one *possessed* suddenly less important than how (and how well) they were *presented*. This exhibitionism reflected a sudden fascination with personality, a concept that, as Samantha Barbas notes, superseded character as the key measure of identity:

> Unlike the nineteenth-century man of character, who cultivated such internal traits as "honesty, truth, nobility and sincerity," the man with personality devoted himself primarily to the art of self-presentation. In a culture based increasingly on appearances and first impressions, he cultivated a pleasing, well groomed appearance . . . and entertained others with his poise and charm . . . He impressed others not with the force of his character, but with his looks, style, humor, and charisma.[7]

Broun's reference to the "camera man behind each tree" is not accidental, for no one was said to master the art of personality better than the film industry's first generation of movie stars. Popular cinematic draws such as Mary Pickford and Douglas Fairbanks even authored advice columns for cultivating personality, teaching fans the acting techniques that allowed them to maximize their unique qualities. Although their recommendations usually revolved around grooming, cosmetics, and elocution, the gurus of self-growth assured readers that they were not advocating artifice. The presentational self did not manufacture personality but externalized innate but untapped traits. Like Broun, however, many commentators impugned the sincerity of these characteristics, associating them with the "ballyhoo" of public relations and advertising. In this way, the performative self raised concern over what exactly constituted an "authentic" identity and to what degree the stylization of behavior turned people into personae.

Had Broun been less irritated by Fitzgerald, he might have appreciated how his fiction explores these questions, often resulting in contradictory conclusions indicative of the confusion they engendered. As we shall see in the next chapter, Fitzgerald often explores the theme of identity through what is called the "concealed identity" motif, by which his heroes adapt alter egos: whether pretending to be a high-seas marauder in "The Offshore Pirate" (1920), a murder suspect in "Rags Jones-Martin and the Pr-nce of W-les," an uncouth beachcomber in "The Unspeakable Egg" (both 1924), or even a mysterious millionaire in *The Great Gatsby* (1925), the ridiculous disguises that Fitzgerald's swains adopt liberate their repressed romanticism. "All my life I have devoted much attention to the so-called niceties of conduct; niceties of dress, of manners, of behavior," declares George Van Tyne in "Egg" after doffing the tramp costume that woos back his disenchanted fiancée, Fifi Marsden. "It was necessary to show [Fifi] what an unspeakable egg I could be."[8] As the plot insists, social constraints repress the real self, which can be expressed only through the paradoxical recourse of role-playing.

The new theatricality also helped to ameliorate traits previously considered indecent, including sexuality. Just as play-acting allowed men like George to overcome the "niceties of conduct" to exude their natural vivacity, so, too, displaying one's sensuality invited a flaunting degree of imagination and exaggeration. One of the flapper's least understood characteristics was her penchant for affectation. As Angela J. Latham notes, her provocative craze for bobbed hair and short skirts was rooted in a self-conscious artificiality: "The 'flapper look' suggested far more than fashionable, immodest, taste in clothing. It comprised a pose, a posturing, a contrived demeanor – in short, a performance."[9] What flappers were "performing," of course, was an unabashed embrace of their sexuality – which is not the same as saying they were sexually active, though moralists proved oblivious to that distinction. By 1921, consternation over the amount of flesh the flapper was willing to expose resulted in

> a number of dress reform efforts . . . including [several by] the YWCA, the Women's Auxiliary of the Episcopal Church, and various state legislatures . . . A bill proposed in Utah, for example, would fine and even imprison women whose skirts were more than three inches above their ankles. An Ohio bill reportedly declared that the skirts of any female over fourteen years of age should reach her instep. Bills proposed in as many as twenty-one states likewise attempted the extraordinary task of measuring modesty by the yard and, as would be expected, yielded results that were anything but consistent. (48)

Fitzgerald parodies this reform hysteria in "Bernice Bobs Her Hair" by noting that the mother of Bernice's potential beau is the author of a recent "paper on 'The Foibles of the Younger Generation' . . . [that] devoted fifteen minutes to bobbed hair. It's her pet abomination" (*Short Stories* 44). He could rib the adult outcry against such licentious fashion trends because he recognized that, as historian Paula S. Fass writes, these fads did not evince "a revolution erupting in a sudden and drastic increase in sexual intercourse among the unmarried young, but a revolution growing out of new patterns of sexual play" that "emphasized several important [generational] value changes," including, most importantly, "the recognition and approval of female sexuality."[10] In other words, what Fass calls the flapper's "purposefully erotic vamp[ing]" (280) provided an exaggerated image that allowed young women to regard their sexuality as a healthy aspect of their personal identity. The tactic of normalizing through display is most apparent in the flapper's fondness for cosmetics, the subject of an early Fitzgerald story, "Sentiment – And the Use of Rouge" (1917), which was subsequently incorporated into *This Side of Paradise*. As Fass notes:

> The use of cosmetics symbolized the woman's open acceptance of her own sexuality . . . By the mores of [Victorian America], cosmetics were immoral. They were associated with prostitutes. By appropriating the right to use such sexual aides, respectable women proclaimed that they too were endowed with a sexual personality. They had taken on themselves as potential wives all the characteristics of lovers. The two kinds of women were no longer separate and distinguishable at first glance but one and the same. (283–4)

Much as Fitzgerald celebrated performative personality, he also cautioned against the identity confusion arising from its theatricality. Throughout *The Great Gatsby* Nick comments on the transparency of his friend's mannerisms, including a masterful paragraph (added at the proof stage) on his supercilious smile, which "understood you just so far as you wanted to be understood, believed in you as you would like to believe in yourself and assured you that it had precisely the impression of you that, at your best, you hoped to convey."[11] Interestingly, Gatsby's repertoire of affectations often *fails* to convey sophistication. Upon reuniting with Daisy for the first time in five years, he leans against a mantelpiece in "a strained counterfeit of perfect ease, even of boredom," a pose of imperturbable cool that crumbles only when in his nervousness he knocks a clock off the shelf (86). Such moments are indicative of Gatsby's naïve assumption that such gesticulations – including his penchant for addressing Nick as "old sport" – will not excite incredulity. In *Tender Is the Night* (1934) Dick Diver has the opposite problem: his gestures erode his sense of self until he is left mimicking the charisma he once effortlessly exuded. In the book's opening Riviera scenes, Rosemary Hoyt is seduced by Dick's charm, which "promised that he would take care of her, and that a little later he would open up whole new worlds for her, unroll an endless succession of magnificent possibilities."[12] Five years later, the dissipated doctor is reduced to attempting water-skiing stunts to impress his former lover, much to Nicole's annoyance: "She knew . . . that he was somewhat tired, that it was only the closeness of Rosemary's exciting youth that prompted the impending effort . . . She wondered coldly if he would make a spectacle of himself" (282–3) – a worry that comes true when Dick repeatedly fails to lift a man on his shoulders, as he could in his prime. Significantly, Dick's last physical action before leaving the Riviera is a gesture: "He raised his right hand and with a papal cross he blessed the beach" (314). Whether this is a sincere abdication of glamor or an ironic admission of defeat remains unclear, suggesting how Fitzgerald was ultimately ambivalent about ostentatious expressions of personality.

The marketplace of self-making: personal style and consumerism

Gestures and poses were not the only media through which people expressed their identities. The expanding consumer market supplied them with what Stuart Ewen calls "style objects," commodities marketed as "images and symbols of luxury, abundance, and distinction, [with] powerful suggestions of privilege and franchise."[13] By choosing from among these accoutrements, the public cultivated a sense of personal style that enabled them to package their personality. The resulting individuality was admittedly paradoxical, given that it was derived through mass-produced goods, yet this contradiction proved less important than the self-making that consumerism promised. As Ewen explains:

> A central appeal of style was its ability to create an illusory transcendence of class or background. While hierarchy and inequities of wealth and power were – in many ways – increasing, the free and open market in style offered a symbolic ability to name oneself; to become a "lady" or a "gentleman," a "Sir" or a "Madam." Mass-produced, often shoddy, style seemed to subvert ancient monopolies. (77)

Fashion is the most obvious mode of style; not surprisingly, Fitzgerald's characters are attentive to the "illusory transcendence" of clothes. The first half of *This Side of Paradise* catalogues Amory's sartorial pretensions, from his first "adult" outfit – "long trousers, set off by a purple accordion tie and a 'Belmont' collar with the edges unassailably meeting, purple socks, and handkerchief with a purple border peeping from the breast pocket"[14] – to the "hand-knit, sleeveless jerseys" he dubs "petting shirts" (60) to his fondness for ruffled silk (64). These dandyish habiliments are integral to his aristocratic image; significantly, when Amory's ambitions are thwarted, references to dress evaporate. Gatsby's parties are likewise pageantries of bourgeois buying power, his "halls and salons and verandas gaudy with primary colors, and hair shorn in strange new ways, and shawls beyond the dreams of Castile" (40). The Day-Glo surrealism of these scenes has much to do with Fitzgerald's eye for color and fabric detail, with women luxuriating in "gas-blue" evening gowns and lavender beads, the men in white flannels, and even a uniform of robin's-egg blue for the chauffeur. Amid this "spectroscopic gayety [*sic*]," old-money attendees attempt to preserve a "dignified homogeneity" by "representing the staid nobility of the countryside – East Egg condescending to West Egg" (44). As Ewen suggests, consumerism erodes the upper-class ability to distinguish itself from the hoi polloi. Far from preserving "staid nobility," these upper-crust emissaries in fact join in Gatsby's revelry – as does Tom Buchanan when he attends a later party. Tom's personal style also suggests how the wealthy accelerate their own "embourgeoisement" – making them "a little less remotely rich" (17), as Nick phrases it – by drawing from the same pool of style objects as the middle class. One of the more curious details in *The Great Gatsby* is Tom's and Daisy's fondness for the *Saturday Evening Post*, which Nick's sometime girlfriend, Jordan Baker, reads aloud to them when bored (20). In the 1920s the *Post* was the veritable bible of middle-class refinement, assuring readers that prosperity entitled them to the same luxuries as the pedigreed classes. The unspoken irony is that Tom, who complains that his social stature is eroding at the hands of the "colored empire," would turn to sources like the *Post* for solace, for it was every bit as responsible for the devaluation of old-money influence as immigration, intermarriage, and other racial phenomena that he blames.

Another style object that altered self-conceptions was the automobile, whose integration into middle-class American life occurred as Fitzgerald's generation came of age. *This Side of Paradise*, early flapper stories, and several Basil and Josephine installments explore the effect of a Blatz Wildcat or a Pierce-Arrow on sexual mores. They also examine the automobile's appeal as a status symbol. "Suddenly the great thing in Basil's crowd was to own an automobile," says "He Thinks He's Wonderful" (1928). "Fun no longer seemed available at great distances, at suburban lakes or remote country clubs. Walking downtown ceased to be a legitimate pastime. On the contrary, a single block from one youth's house to another's must be navigated in a car. Dependent groups formed around owners and they began to wield what was, to Basil at least, a disconcerting power."[15]

More subtly, Fitzgerald uses the automobile to suggest how, thanks to consumerism, human interaction was becoming more mechanical and, paradoxically, more undisciplined. A persistent motif is the interfolding of man and machine. Whether through *The Great Gatsby*'s depiction of the "throbbing taxis" of New York – borrowed from T. S. Eliot's *The Waste Land* (1922) – or the gruesome sight of Myrtle Wilson's breast "swinging loose like a flap" after being struck by Gatsby's coupé, Fitzgerald alternately evokes anthropomorphic and dehumanized images that suggest that the boundaries between subject and object are indistinct. (The point is also made through the use of brand names for characters; Jordan Baker is an amalgam of two competing automobiles.) Yet Fitzgerald also associated vehicles with carelessness and irresponsibility through the many wrecks in his fiction. In addition to Myrtle, Dick Humbird in *This Side of Paradise* is killed while drink-driving, while lesser accidents in both *The Beautiful and Damned* and *Tender Is the Night* dramatize the moral recklessness of Gloria Patch and Nicole Diver. What links these seemingly opposing motifs is the era's anxiety over consumer detachment: whatever freedoms it provided, the automobile contributed to the technological routinization of life, which in turn encouraged and excused the ethical callousness that Jordan embodies when she lies about leaving the top of a borrowed car down in the rain or when she passes "so close to some workman that [her] fender flicked a button on one man's coat" (57–8).

Flaunting recreations: conspicuous leisure and the culture of indulgence

A related development Fitzgerald explored was the emergence of a leisure culture that challenged the Protestant work ethic by insisting that entertainment, not productive labor, was life's main aim. One arena in which this phenomenon flourished was that of the decade's many fads, whether mah-jong, beauty contests, flagpole sitting, or tanning (a minor motif in *Tender Is the Night*). Of course, there were crazes before the 1920s, but the speed with which the media could now popularize them guaranteed an unprecedented visibility. Additionally, they were practiced with a new conspicuousness, becoming public spectacles designed to attract attention and generate controversy. It is hard to think of a tamer amusement than the crossword puzzle, yet even that attained the *sine qua non* of notoriety when "a man [was] sent to jail for refusing to leave a restaurant after four hours of trying to solve a puzzle."[16] An arrest was an important mark of distinction for Jazz Age leisure because it registered society's main objection: recreational activities promoted an ethos of pure fun rather than self-improvement, encouraging indulgence instead of rectitude.

Characteristically, Fitzgerald's fiction both delights in and disapproves of this mindset. He depicts the sensual glee of dancing, which was "unquestionably the most popular social pastime" of the era – and thus one of the most controversial:

"The dancers were close, the steps were fast, and the music was jazz. And because popular forms of dancing were intimate and contorting, and the music was rhythmic and throbbing, it called down upon itself all the venom of offended respectability" (*American Youth* 301). Whether the intimacy of the foxtrot or that of the tango, Fitzgerald suggests how the choreographies of dance and sex were often indistinguishable, as when Dick and Rosemary take to the floor in *Tender Is the Night*: "He turned her here and there with such a delicacy of suggestion that she was like a bright bouquet, a piece of precious cloth being displayed before fifty eyes. There was a moment when they were not dancing at all, simply clinging together" (76–7). True to every moralist who feared that dancing aroused libidinous desires, Dick and Rosemary quickly ensconce themselves in the coatroom. Yet Fitzgerald was less enthusiastic about such scandalous steps as the black bottom, the turkey trot, and the shimmy, viewing them as emblematic of narcissistic exhibitionism. (Surprisingly, he gives the era's most famous dance craze, the Charleston, little attention.) At Gatsby's parties Nick is startled by the "confident girls" who become the center of attention by "dancing individualistically" (46), including one who "seizes a cocktail out of the air, dumps it down for courage and, moving her hands like Frisco, dances alone on the canvas platform" (41). As Anthony J. Berret has shown, several Basil and Josephine stories also voice concern over the innuendo of modern dances. In "The Perfect Life" (1929) the young hero observes "all ages and several classes of society shuffl[ing] around tensely to the nervous, disturbing beats of 'Too Much Mustard,'" whose lyrics testify to dance's salacious appeal: "Tango makes you warm inside; / You bend and sway and glide; / There's nothing far and wide – " (*Basil and Josephine* 166, 168).[17]

An even more controversial pastime that raised concerns about the new leisure culture was drinking. Never mind that as of January 16, 1920, Prohibition rendered alcohol illegal; neither the Eighteenth Amendment nor the Volstead Act (the amendment's legal enforcement) curbed consumption. "The popular concept of the 'Roaring Twenties' as a time when everyone danced the Charleston until dawn in speakeasies and swigged hooch out of silver flasks is pure myth," insists one recent historian. "Speakeasies and the cocktail hour were unknown to a majority of Americans." Nevertheless, those same everyday folk felt little compunction about disobeying the law, thus creating a black market bootlegging industry that supported a range of illicit manufacturers, "from the corner grocer selling pints of bathtub gin out the side door, to such giants of the profession as Al Capone" and Arnold Rothstein, the model for *The Great Gatsby*'s Meyer Wolfsheim.[18] Less obviously, the illicitness of alcohol helped to foster a binge mentality in which intoxication became another performative spectacle. Previously, public drunkenness had been associated with the poor and the working class, but being visibly "tight" was now a rite (and right) of prosperity. As a result, Fitzgerald's characters do not merely revel in the joys of getting "stewed" – they want to be *observed* doing it, their uninhibited behavior a testament to both the thrill of irresponsibility and their need for attention. This latter desire explains why a theatrical strain runs throughout scenes of intemperance. In "May Day" (1920) Philip Dean and Peter Himmel turn into veritable vaudevillians the drunker they get, nicknaming themselves "Mr. In" and "Mr. Out" as they irritate waiters, taxi drivers, and doormen. As Himmel says as the pair pelt patrons with food at a fashionable breakfast eatery, "'Thank you for your kind applause, ladies and gentlemen. If some one will lend me some more hash and a tall hat we will go on with the act'" (*Short Stories* 134). Similarly, the Divers' inebriated adventures in Paris are described as a "slapstick comedy," with Abe North passing himself off as General Pershing to commandeer champagne from the Ritz Hotel and Rosemary climbing atop a market wagon of carrots to ride through the streets. Rosemary's vision of Dick as the master of these ceremonies likewise suggests how alcohol inspires such spectacles: "The enthusiasm, the selflessness behind the whole performance ravished her" (77–8).

Of course, Fitzgerald's fiction comments upon any number of other 1920s trends, from the emergence of modern music (including – obviously enough – jazz) to the rise of communism, fascism, and other political ideologies. What links these disparate phenomena to youth, consumerism, and leisure is their redefinition of the possibilities of selfhood. Even in his breeziest works, Fitzgerald devoted himself to gauging the effect of cultural change on the individual. As such, his fiction does not merely offer a vivid portrait of his era; it represents a reckoning, an effort to understand the moral shading that separates opportunity from temptation.

Works

A good starting point for understanding Fitzgerald is a passage from his 1933 essay "One Hundred False Starts":

> Mostly, we authors must repeat ourselves – that's the truth. We have two or three great and moving experiences in our lives – experiences so great and moving that it doesn't seem at the time that anyone else has been so caught up and pounded and dazzled and astonished and beaten and broken and rescued and illuminated and rewarded and humbled in just that way ever before.
>
> Then we learn our trade, well or less well, and we tell our two or three stories – each time in a new disguise – maybe ten times, maybe a hundred, as long as people will listen.[1]

Initially, this seems a rather defensive rebuttal to charges that Fitzgerald's interests were narrow and repetitive. Yet the real concern is not his supposed lack of range (an accusation most writers suffer) but the pressures of earning a living. "For eighteen years," the author insists, "writing has been my chief interest in life, and I am in every sense a professional" (*Afternoon of an Author* 131). While that description may not jibe with his image, it is important to remember that he was the only major author of the 1920s other than Sinclair Lewis (1885–1951) to live exclusively by writing.[2] Financial considerations dictated that few artistic choices were made without considering the marketplace. And yet Fitzgerald could never view his work objectively as true professionalism demands. Contemporaries such as Ben Hecht (1894–1964), Anita Loos (1889–1981), and Elinor Glyn (1864–1943) – all of whom drew Fitzgerald comparisons – were more prolific because they could operate with a cool efficiency of craft. By contrast, Fitzgerald could complete a story or novel only when compelled by its personal significance: "I must start out with an emotion," he admits, explaining why so many entries in the "leather-bound wastebasket which I fatuously refer to as my 'notebook'" fail to come to fruition, "one that's close to me and that I can understand" (*Afternoon of an Author* 132).

Fitzgerald's struggle to finesse the divide between the artist and the professional writer accounts for much of his uniqueness. Although, unlike Ezra Pound (1885–1972), T. S. Eliot, and James Joyce (1882–1941), he never obscured his personality behind a façade of experimentation, he was fluent in the techniques of such high modernist masterpieces as *Hugh Selwyn Mauberley* (1920), *The Waste Land* (1922), and *Ulysses* (1922). At the same time, the rejection slips he accumulated during his 1919 apprenticeship taught him the economic necessity of knowing the conventions of mass-market fiction – which, fortunately, were compatible with his talents. Even the most ridiculed aspect of 1920s popular writing, its emotional expressiveness, suited his literary instincts; as Matthew J. Bruccoli writes, Fitzgerald's "rationale of style was to multiply meaning through lyrical language, and the liquefaction of his prose becomes an incantation"[3] – a rationale as apparent in stories conceived strictly for cash as in *The Great Gatsby* (1925).

Most studies of Fitzgerald analyze his writing chronologically, dividing his career into four stages: his popular peak (1920–5), his post-*Gatsby* indirection (1926–31), his *Tender Is the Night/Crack-Up* decline (1932–6), and his final Hollywood years (1937–40). Yet such an approach views his work strictly through the prism of personal ups and downs, overshadowing the artistry. The following overview is thus a topical survey, examining his composition process; his major themes, characters, and plots; the literary modes and genres he practiced; and his style. Apropos of "One Hundred False Starts," this approach emphasizes Fitzgerald's professionalism, demonstrating that his legacy lies in the literature, not the legend.

Composition process

Eschewing biographical interpretation does not mean ignoring Fitzgerald's work habits, for understanding how an author writes is often as illuminating as studying his subject matter. Indeed, in Fitzgerald's case analyzing the composition process reveals a vital yet unappreciated fact: his fiction was the product of assiduous effort – not, as his reputation would suggest, hasty effusions from a glib talent. "They said he had 'fatal facility,'" Fitzgerald complains in

"Afternoon of an Author" (1936), referring to himself in the third person. "[Yet] he labored like a slave over every sentence so as not to be like that" (*Afternoon of an Author* 181). His manuscripts corroborate his conscientious craftsmanship. Even in his commercial stories, "there was one little drop of something not blood, not a tear, not my seed, but me more intimately than these, in every story, it was the extra I had."[4]

As previously noted, "One Hundred False Starts" refers to Fitzgerald's notebook, which he calls his "leather-bound wastebasket" because of its abundance of stillborn story ideas. Yet the description of this "clot of pages" is misleading, for he did not itemize such dubious plots as "The Winter Was Cold" and "Dog: The Story of a Little Dog." Nor did it play the role in his creative process that he claims. Typically, a writer's notebook serves as part-diary and part-repository of possible inspiration, with random observations, plot kernels, and newspaper clippings filed for future use. While both Nathaniel Hawthorne (1804–1864) and Henry James (1843–1916) relied heavily on journals for this purpose, no significant Fitzgerald work evolved à la "Wakefield" (1835) or "The Altar of the Dead" (1895). In fact, it appears that Fitzgerald did not even maintain a formal notebook until 1932, when he hired typists to organize his scattered notes. Instead, almost all of his fiction originated from the same source as his 1932 *Saturday Evening Post* story "One Interne," whose genesis "One Hundred False Starts" recounts: "Last summer I was hauled to the hospital with a tentative diagnosis of typhoid . . . Three days after I was discharged I had finished a story about a hospital" (*Afternoon of an Author* 133). In other words, Fitzgerald's most fruitful source of inspiration was personal experience.

It was a dependency that critics did not fail to notice. "He can not create beyond himself nor imagine experience very different from his own," Harvey Eagleton complained in 1925. "He is continuously autobiographic . . . [W]hen he cannot think of a simple plot on which he can hang his experience, he writes articles about himself and sells them to the *American Magazine,* the *Saturday Evening Post,* and the *Women's Home Companion.*"[5] If Eagleton sounds irritated, it is because at the peak of his fame Fitzgerald so flaunted the connection between his life and his writing that the resulting façade of self-absorption became a defining facet of his literary persona. In 1958 *The Smart Set* co-editor George Jean Nathan remembered the author reneging on a promise to make him a major character in *The Beautiful and Damned* (1922): "He came to me somewhat apologetically and explained that he had tried, but could not lionize me in his novel. He said that he found himself unable to write a heroic character other than himself and that he had to be the hero of any novel he undertook."[6] Yet interpreting Fitzgerald's protagonists as versions of himself underestimates the amount of imaginative transformation that went into his fiction. While the autobiographical impetus behind a certain plot or motif is often easily identified, his works usually deviate from authorial actualities to serve a literary purpose.

Consider "'The Sensible Thing,'" whose 1924 revisiting of Scott's and Zelda's courtship after *This Side of Paradise* (1920), "The Ice Palace" (1920), *The Beautiful and Damned*, and several earlier retellings has long been considered expedient rather than artistic, mainly because it was one of the dozen stories written to finance work on *The Great Gatsby* (1925). Although Fitzgerald collected the story in *All the Sad Young Men* (1926), he seems to have had no special affection for it, dismissing it to Maxwell Perkins as "about Zelda + me. All true."[7] The claim is curious, however, for the plot departs from the Fitzgeralds' romance in important ways, not the least of which is that the young lovers, George O'Kelly and Jonquil Cary, do not marry. While George, not unlike Fitzgerald, enjoys an unexpected reversal of fortune that makes him financially suitable for Jonquil, he recognizes that the love that compelled him to prove his worthiness has diminished: "For an instant as he kissed her he knew that though he search through eternity he could never recapture those lost April hours . . . Well, let it pass, he thought; April is over, April is over. There are all kinds of love in the world, but never the same love twice."[8]

Alice Hall Petry has suggested that this ending allowed Fitzgerald to ponder the degree of resolve he would have needed in 1919 to break from the noncommittal Zelda: "Though '"The Sensible Thing"' records many of the details of the Scott/Zelda courtship, it is more accurately seen as an imaginative recreation of that courtship – one with, in retrospect, a 'happy' ending: no marriage, and the man's free will intact."[9] Yet the significance of George's stoic self-counsel is not limited to Fitzgerald's marital regrets. In thematic terms, George's acceptance of passion's transience represents an ongoing attempt to catalogue the different emotional responses to the disparity between idealism and reality. Love in Fitzgerald always occasions some degree of loss, and his beaux cope differently with it. George's relative placidity can be plotted on the resigned (some would say mature) side of a continuum whose extremes are defined by Dexter Green in "Winter Dreams" (1922), who bemoans love's passing in a threnody ("The dream was gone. Something had been taken from him . . . The gates were closed, the sun was gone down, and there was no beauty but the gray beauty of steel that withstands all time. Even the grief he could have borne was left behind in the country of illusion, of youth, of the richness of life, where his winter dreams had flourished" [*Short Stories* 145]) and Jay Gatsby, who maintains an "inviolable" belief in Daisy right up to his murder ("Can't repeat the past? Of course you can!" [107]). As its title suggests, "'The Sensible Thing'" is about cultivating what Petry calls a "self-protective strategy" toward romance, one that, by "acknowledg[ing] that time changes all things, including love," would enable an idealist "to tolerate more readily whatever disappointments . . . he will encounter in his life" (139–40). As such, Fitzgerald was not merely returning to a pivotal personal event out of a paucity of material or because stories of young love (even sad ones) were saleable. He was exploring alternative reactions to what he viewed as the most fundamental of human experiences: loss.

Nor, as Eagleton claims, was Fitzgerald incapable of "creat[ing] beyond himself." Nathan's experience notwithstanding, his interest in character often led him to appropriate the personalities of close friends. Anson Hunter, the protagonist of "The Rich Boy" (1926), was modeled on Princeton friend Ludlow Fowler (1897–1961), who was so startled to discover himself a case study in emotional detachment that he requested changes in incriminating details before the story appeared in *Redbook* (1926). (They were not made until *All the Sad Young Men*). Even more famously, early drafts of *Tender Is the Night* (1934) were intended as portraits of Gerald and Sara Murphy, the Fitzgeralds' Riviera hosts in the mid-1920s. Although Dick and Nicole Diver (originally Seth and Dinah Piper/Roreback) eventually metamorphosed into versions of Scott and Zelda, the Divers' magnetism in Book I owes much to the Murphys' regal sophistication. Sara Murphy was particularly irritated by Fitzgerald's literary surveillance: "You can't expect anyone to like or stand a *Continual* feeling of analysis + sub-analysis + criticism," she complained. "*You ought to know at your age that you can't have theories about friends.*"[10]

The Hollywood titan Irving Thalberg died before Fitzgerald based *The Last Tycoon*'s (1941) Monroe Stahr on him, yet the author was nervous enough about his intentions being misperceived that he drafted a letter to Thalberg's widow, the actress Norma Shearer (1900–1983): "Though the story is imaginary perhaps you could see it as an attempt to preserve something of Irving. My own impression shortly recorded but very dazzling in its effect on me, inspired the best part of the character of Stahr – though I have put in some things drawn from other men and, inevitably, much of myself."[11] And while Ernest Hemingway routinely disparaged Fitzgerald by 1934–5, his condescension did not stop his rival from translating his mercurial swagger to a medieval prince named Philippe for a prospective historical novel called *The Castle*. "Just as Stendahl's [*sic*] portrait of a Byronic man made *Le Rouge et Noir* so couldn't my portrait of Ernest as Phillipe [*sic*] make the real modern man?" Fitzgerald wondered while conceiving the character (*Notebooks* 159).

Similarly, not all plots were autobiographical. Fitzgerald was not in attendance at the 1919 Christmas party at the St Paul home of railroad heir Louis Hill at which a crasher named Eddie Saunders promenaded about in a dromedary costume. Nevertheless, the incident inspired one of his most popular early stories, "The Camel's Back" (1920). A lesser-known effort, "The Intimate Strangers" (1935), was based on the marriage of North Carolina friends Lefty and Nora Flynn, while "The End of Hate" (1940) drew from Edward Fitzgerald's Civil War boyhood. In rare cases literary sources even provided plotlines. "Tarquin of Cheapside" (1917; revised 1921 and retitled "Tarquin of Cheapside") purports to tell how Shakespeare came to write "The Rape of Lucrece," while "The Third Casket" (1924) updates *The Merchant of Venice*. While his life may have provided his most memorable material, these examples demonstrate that Fitzgerald was not as "continuously autobiographic" as assumed.

After formulating a scenario or plot, Fitzgerald proceeded to the drafting stage, which for him was virtually indistinguishable from what for most authors is a separate third step in the writing process: revision. Because he did not work on a typewriter, he hired secretaries to produce typed copies of handwritten manuscript that he would then rewrite while embarking upon new sections of text. This was particularly true with his novels, which, for obvious reasons, posed more complicated structuring challenges than shorter works. In fact, one reason why Fitzgerald proved so prolific as a short-story writer was that his "best story ideas came to him as complete structures, and by writing them in concentrated bursts of effort" – such as the single day's labor he claimed it took to complete "The Camel's Back" – "he was able to preserve the spontaneity of the narrative" (*Epic Grandeur* 131). His term for narrative structure was "jump," the most intricate of which was the "three-jump story," so named because it could be completed "in three successive days." Speed and ease of completion were necessary to preserve the organicism of the plot: "In many stories one strikes a snag that must be hacked at but on the whole, stories that drag along or are terribly difficult (I mean a difficulty that comes from a poor conception and consequent faulty construction) never flow quite as well in the reading."[12]

What actually prevents "drag" in his stories is a dramatic form known as Freytag's pyramid. Fitzgerald need not have studied Gustav Freytag's *Technique of the Drama* (1863) to be familiar with the German novelist's five-part prescription for narrative structure. By the mid-1920s, the idea that a story should develop from exposition to rising action to a dramatic climax before descending through falling action into a denouement had provided the template for commercial fiction. Fitzgerald's first *Saturday Evening Post* contribution, "Head and Shoulders" (1920), offers a convenient example. The opening section introduces the two protagonists, the genius-phenom Horace Tarbox and the chorus girl Marcia Meadow. The second and third detail their budding romance, which occasions a gradual switching of personalities, culminating in the fourth part with a climactic twist: to solve their financial problems (the couple are newly married), Horace abandons his unprofitable studies to work as a circus acrobat, while, unbeknown to him, Marcia writes a piece of "immortally illiterate literature" entitled *Samuel Pepys, Syncopated.* "'Trying to choose our mediums and then taking what we get,'" marvels Horace at the irony of their role reversal. "'And being glad'" (*Short Stories* 22). The denouement describes how Marcia's bestselling book wins kudos by drawing praise from French philosopher Anton Laurier, whom Horace once sought to impress but who now hails Marcia as the family prodigy. What makes the story satisfying is the farcical completeness of this turnabout; one may anticipate Marcia costing Horace his intellectual agility, but not until Laurier's surprise appearance does one really appreciate the intricacy of the mismatched lovers' comic opposition.

Other *Saturday Evening Post* tales adopt Freytag's format without seeming formulaic, thanks to Fitzgerald's talent for witty and often preposterous plot twists. By contrast, his 1930s stories proved harder to sell because Fitzgerald no longer conceived storylines as completed structures, and his drafts lost dramatic unity. He recognized this in 1939 when he explained the failings of "The End of Hate," which went through innumerable revisions before *Collier's* editor Kenneth Littauer unenthusiastically accepted it: "Finishing this story was a somewhat harder job than writing *Tender Is the Night*," Fitzgerald decided, "because (a) when the conception goes wrong repair work is twice as hard as building a new story and (b) because the 5,000 word length is terribly difficult . . . it means [a] forshortening [*sic*] of plot into melodrama."[13] The effort Fitzgerald invested in structuring his stories debunks one of the more dubious legends of his career – one, perhaps not surprisingly, perpetuated by Hemingway: "He told me . . . how he wrote what he thought were good stories, and which really were good stories for the *Post*, and then changed them for submission, knowing exactly how he must make the twists that made them salable magazine stories."[14] Simply put, this is a spurious claim. No manuscript evidence finds Fitzgerald doing intentional damage to enhance his stories' commerciality; even when resorting to formulae, his aim was to avoid contrivance and respect the integrity of the original idea.

This point is further corroborated by the role that Fitzgerald's stories played in his novel writing, which was to provide "a workshop for subjects, themes, and techniques that he would continue to develop."[15] Especially with more commercial stories, "Fitzgerald's practice . . . was to copy memorable phrases, sentences, and paragraphs . . . into his notebooks. These gleanings he then considered eligible for reuse in his novels. Tearsheets of the stories (the printed texts, torn from the magazine issues) would be placed in his files with the legend '*Positively not to be republished in any form!*' written across the top of the first page" ("Professional Author" 57). Thus a transitional paragraph in "Diamond

Dick and the First Law of Woman" (1924) reappears in *The Great Gatsby*, where its lugubrious sonority conveys Daisy Buchanan's romantic appeal: "For Daisy was young and her artificial world was redolent of orchids and pleasant, cheerful snobbery and orchestras which set the rhythm of the year, summing up the sadness and suggestiveness of life in new tunes."[16] Similarly, Amanthis Powell's passing comment in "Dice, Brass Knuckles & Guitar" (1923) becomes, for narrator Nick Carraway, *Gatsby*'s most emphatic critique of the moral dubiety of the rich: "You're worth the whole damn bunch put together" (122). The novel containing the greatest number of these "strippings" is *Tender Is the Night* – not surprising, given that Fitzgerald wrote nearly sixty stories in the decade between *Gatsby* and *Tender*. Thirty-seven different stories contributed to *Tender*, dating as far back as 1922's "The Popular Girl." Many of these passages are descriptive and help to create *Tender*'s hallucinatory atmosphere. An interior monologue from "Flight and Pursuit" (1932) is recast to convey Nicole Diver's fragile thought process: "Dress stay crisp for him, button stay put, bloom narcissus – air stay still and sweet."[17] Other borrowings are far more extensive, including fifteen different passages from "Jacob's Ladder" (1927). Exploring how the same sentence functions in different contexts is an illuminating exercise; it is a testament to Fitzgerald's ability to create unique dramatis personae that descriptions of Jenny Prince, the heroine of "Jacob's Ladder," are transferred to both Nicole and Rosemary Hoyt without blurring their distinctiveness.

Because Fitzgerald's novels were not conceived as unified "jumps," with the major exception of *The Great Gatsby* their plots unfold episodically rather than through dramatic complications and twists. The rounds of revisions that ran deep into the galley stage typically addressed style more than story construction, for "in revising, Fitzgerald was chiefly interested in the movement of his sentences and in the accuracy and vividness of his descriptive phrases. Only rarely did he alter the organization of a paragraph – and almost never did he revise for meaning. But he was endlessly patient about trying to make a sentence more graceful or striking."[18] The preference for polish over structure accounts for yet another animadversion that Fitzgerald has suffered, best voiced by Albert Lubell in a 1955 critique of *Tender Is the Night*: "The novel . . . suffers from an all but fatal diffuseness, which can only be explained by the author's lack of control over his material. Whatever unity the novel possesses is one of tone and mood, resulting largely from Fitzgerald's style" (qtd. in *Composition* 12). The charge is curious, given that "diffuseness" was actually a modernist aim. From Joyce to Virginia Woolf and even Hemingway, plotting was deemed more appropriate for melodramatic potboilers than literature, whose proper concern was consciousness and character. Like these peers, Fitzgerald considered unity a matter of atmosphere, not story logic. Until the end of his career, he never formally outlined his novels, preferring to assemble them according to "general plans" and statements of purpose. When he did chart their structure, he was concerned with proportion, not the sequence of events, projecting word lengths for chapters to ensure shape and form.

This is not to say that Fitzgerald is innocent of digression and inconsistency – merely that instances of them are usually products of haste rather than ineptitude. First-time readers of *This Side of Paradise* are often struck by its miscellany feel, which inspired some reviewers to speculate that the book had been dashed off in a single gust of inspiration. In reality, its patchwork quality reflects the fact that it was partly compiled by splicing together portions of his rejected 1918 "The Romantic Egotist" manuscript, short stories ("Babes in the Woods," 1917; revised 1919), plays ("The Débutante," 1917; revised 1919), and even undergraduate verse. The *New Republic* was not off the mark in dubbing *Paradise* "the collected works of F. Scott Fitzgerald published in novel form."[19]

Although an August 1921 *St Paul Daily News* headline announced that Fitzgerald was outlining new novels, no evidence suggests that he formally planned the sprawling plot of *The Beautiful and Damned*. His initial ambition was to further exaggerate *This Side of Paradise*'s grab-bag format by stringing together various "cynical incidents" he could first sell in "units separately to different magazines, as I write them" (*As Ever* 9). He abandoned this approach at the encouragement of novelist Shane Leslie (who had originally recommended him to Scribner's): "I'm taking your advice and writing very slowly and paying much attention to form," Fitzgerald wrote to Leslie in late 1920. "Sometimes I think this new novel has nothing much else but form" (*Letters* 377). There is much truth to this remark, though not in the way Fitzgerald intended. While attempting to teach himself structure, he inscribed his frustrations into the story via intrusive commentary that, under the guise of character analysis, justifies plot points. In what should be *Beautiful*'s complicating apex, Anthony Patch's wealthy grandfather, Adam, unexpectedly appears at one of Anthony's and Gloria's drunken parties and, disgusted by the depravity, immediately disinherits the couple. Instead of dramatizing the Patches' shock at losing their fortune, Fitzgerald indulges in a windy account of their awareness that for some time "things had been slipping perceptibly." The sole purpose of this digression is to convince the reader that such a spoiled pair are capable of the remorse that the advancing plot demands: "In Gloria had been born something that she had hitherto never needed – the skeleton . . . of her ancient abhorrence, a conscience . . . After Adam Patch's unexpected call, they awoke, nauseated and tired, dispirited with life, capable only of one pervasive emotion – fear."[20] Although Fitzgerald would later admit that "I devoted so much more care to the *detail* of the book than I did to thinking out the *general* scheme," his habit of explaining events suggests that he was constructing his scheme *through* that detail (*A Life in Letters* 61).

Fitzgerald claimed that he revised *The Beautiful and Damned* extensively after its serialization in *Metropolitan Magazine* began in September 1921. Yet the changes were again stylistic rather than substantive: "Almost every page was revised, but the published novel did not alter the plot or structure of the novel" (*Epic Grandeur* 182). The major alteration involved the ending, which originally climaxed with a grandiloquent tribute to Anthony's and Gloria's romantic naïveté: "In the search for happiness, which is the greatest and possibly the only crime of which we in our petty misery are capable, these two people were marked as guilty chiefly by the freshness and fullness of their desire" (qtd. in *Epic Grandeur* 183). At Zelda's urging Fitzgerald opted for a more satiric conclusion in which the Patches regain their inheritance after an exhausting court battle, only to forget that their character flaws, not outside forces, were their ruin: "'I showed them,'" Anthony declares, oblivious to the wheelchair to which he is confined. "'It was a hard fight, but I didn't give up and I came through!'" (449). Whatever the revision gained in verbal economy was obscured by the ambiguity of authorial motive, for the new ending negated the moral reckoning demanded by the Patches' downfall. Perkins described one confused reader's response: "I received the comment that Anthony was unscathed; that he came through with his millions, and thinking well of himself. This man completely missed the extraordinary effective irony of the last few paragraphs."[21] Such confusion was understandable, however, for the revisions failed to establish a consistent attitude toward the Patches, who are alternately romanticized and condemned. Glaring minor details also revealed Fitzgerald's struggle with what he called the "bugbear of inconsistency"; thanks to a letter from admirer George A. Kuyper, he was horrified to discover that he had set Gloria's birthday in three different months (*Correspondence* 98).

While conceiving *The Great Gatsby*, Fitzgerald recognized that he must avoid the structural flaws of *This Side of Paradise* and *The Beautiful and Damned* if he were "to write something *new* – something extraordinary and simple and beautiful + intricately patterned," as he outlined his ambitions in July 1922 (*Correspondence* 112). Doing so required discarding a 1923 false start set in the 1880s involving Catholicism. Unfortunately, this initial draft does not survive except for two handwritten pages and "Absolution" (1924), an 18,000-word story. The first completed version of *Gatsby*, written between April and November 1924 during the Fitzgeralds' Riviera stay, does survive to reveal how, for the first time, he was willing to reorder scenes in order to build suspense and mystery. Originally, for example, Nick Carraway's first encounter with the elusive Gatsby occurred in Chapter II instead of Chapter III. Only after describing the mysterious millionaire's parties and Nick's introduction to the Jewish gangster Meyer Wolfsheim (the novel's eventual fourth chapter) did he conceive Nick's meeting with Tom Buchanan's mistress, Myrtle Wilson, which in the manuscript is placed after Gatsby's party and the Wolfsheim encounter instead of before them. This initial ordering demystifies Gatsby by introducing him too early. The adjoining of Nick's two separate trips into New York also deflates the dramatic impact of each. As he reorganized these plot events, Fitzgerald also shifted melodic paragraphs to enhance their rhetorical effect. For example, the novel's closing "against the current" oratory – his most quoted lines – originally appeared at the end of Chapter I.

Upon receiving *The Great Gatsby* in late 1924, Maxwell Perkins praised the style but suggested revisions that would account for the hero's wealth without detracting from its intrigue: "You might here and there interpolate some phrases, and possibly incidents, little touches of various kinds, that would suggest that he was in some active way mysteriously engaged . . . What Gatsby did ought never to be definitely imparted . . . [but] if some sort of business activity of his were simply adumbrated, it would lend further probability to that part of the story" (*Dear Scott/Dear Max* 83–4). Perkins was probably shocked by the amount of revision Fitzgerald undertook, for instead of "interpolating" hints, he restructured significant amounts of material. (An unrevised version of these galleys, published in 2000 as *Trimalchio* – one of the novel's working titles – allows these changes to be tracked.) The original penultimate chapter included a long account of Gatsby's background, including his real name, James Gatz, and how he came to love Daisy: "'I'll tell you everything,' he broke out exuberantly. 'The whole story. I've never told it to anyone before – not even Daisy.'"[22] Fitzgerald moved a portion of this backstory to the beginning of Chapter VI, where it builds tension by only *gradually* introducing the audience to the facts behind the hero's "secret extravaganza" (148). The change required a wholesale rewriting of Chapters VI and VII, at which point Fitzgerald also deleted exchanges in which Gatsby reveals too much of himself: "'I'm only thirty-two. I might be a great man if I could forget that once I lost Daisy. But my career has got to . . . keep going up'" (90).

Another element Fitzgerald enhanced was Nick's ethical affinity with Gatsby. As James L. W. West III notes, in *Trimalchio* Nick "is not quite so likable or self-deprecating, and he more obviously controls the narrative. His love affair with Jordan Baker is traced in greater detail, and we see more readily why they are attracted to each other" (*Trimalchio* xviii). By depicting his narrator as less of an active agent and more of a witness, Fitzgerald made Nick's assessment of Gatsby as ambiguous as Gatsby's character; ultimately, Nick is as much of an enigma to readers as Gatsby is to him. The rewriting that transformed *Trimalchio* into *The Great Gatsby* was not, as the author claimed, "one of the most expensive affairs since [Flaubert revised] Madame Bovary," yet it nevertheless proved central to the novel's aesthetic success (*Dear Scott/Dear Max* 89). Had Fitzgerald not been willing to undertake such uncharacteristically extensive revision, *Gatsby* would not have ended up quite so great.

Although *The Great Gatsby* was not a commercial success, its artistry inspired Fitzgerald to attempt an even more ambitious novel, "something really NEW in form, idea, structure – the model for the age that Joyce and Stein are searching for, that Conrad didn't find" (*A Life in Letters* 108). Yet the manuscript he labored over for the next four years bears little evidence of innovation. In drafting the story of an American expatriate, Francis Melarky, whose dissolution culminates in matricide, Fitzgerald seems to have adapted events from his own life without any overarching sense of how to cohere his plot. A prologue in which Melarky is arrested in Rome after drunkenly brawling with cabdrivers was based on Fitzgerald's own humiliating 1925 beating by Italian police. A later chapter in which Melarky attends a garden party hosted by Seth and Dinah Roreback (or Piper; Fitzgerald was undecided about the surname) conveys the enchantment of Gerald's and Sara Murphy's "many fetes." With these scenes he combined more sensational material, including a farcical duel between Riviera hangers-on and incidents documenting the rage that was to lead Melarky to murder his mother, Charlotte. The revisions that occupied much of 1926 but thereafter only sporadic intervals until the Melarky plot was abandoned in 1929–30 show these episodes recombined in different orders, as if Fitzgerald were shuffling cards hoping to discover a convincing sequence. His inability to progress beyond these initial scenes may again reflect the episodic nature of his composition process: in November 1928 he promised to submit two chapters per month to Perkins, believing that a writing schedule would "help me get [the plot] straight in my own mind – I've been alone with it too long" (*A Life in Letters* 159). Yet, without a clear sense of direction, he was unable to complete new installments, and the plan fell apart after only one submission.

Perhaps inspired by "The Rough Crossing," a June 1929 *Saturday Evening Post* story about an expatriate couple's stormy marriage, Fitzgerald briefly reconceived his novel, replacing the matricide plot with an adultery triangle involving movie director Lew Kelly, his wife Nicole, and an aspiring actress named Rosemary. Yet this version also petered out after two chapters, and he returned to Melarky, hoping again to complete it by submitting monthly chapters – this time to Harold Ober. This scheme proved unfeasible as well, albeit for an understandable reason: shortly thereafter, Zelda suffered her first breakdown, and her subsequent hospitalization halted his novel writing for nearly two years.

By summer 1932, Fitzgerald recognized that if he were ever to complete the book he needed to formalize his composition process. Accordingly, he prepared a "General Plan" to guide his work, a technique inspired by a description of Emile Zola's literary procedure in Matthew Josephson's *Zola and His Time* (1928). Significantly, Fitzgerald's sixteen-page document does not include a formal plot outline; although it begins with a declaration of intent ("The novel should do this. Show a man who is a natural idealist, a spoiled priest, giving in for various causes to the ideas of the haute Bourgeoise [*sic*]") and sketches the basic storyline, it does not chart the action chapter by chapter. Rather, his notes are character sketches for the recast Pipers/Rorebacks/Kellys, now called Dick and Nicole Diver. In Dick's case the descriptions are abstractly philosophical, suggesting that Fitzgerald cared less about plotting his hero's decay than in clarifying his symbolic significance. Thus the dissipating psychiatrist "is a superman in possibilities, that is, he appears to be at first sight from a burgeoise [*sic*] point of view. However he lacks that tensile strength – none of the ruggedness of Brancusi, Leger, Picasso." Nicole's material, meanwhile, compiles details drawn from Zelda's breakdown, including one page devoted to the "parallel between actual case and case in novel": "A woman of 29 has a rivalry complex for success and power competing with her husband," reads the first box in the Zelda column. "A girl of 15 has a father complex deliberately built up by her father, a well-screened diagnosis," reads the corresponding entry for Nicole. As this example suggests, while Nicole generally resembled Zelda, she was also distinctly fictional, especially as regards her incestuous relationship with her father. The plan also reveals that Fitzgerald felt that personal experience alone would not ensure an accurate treatment of mental illness; a section entitled "Method of Dealing with Sickness Material" includes an admonishment to "[be] careful not to reveal basic ignorance of psychiatric and medical training yet not being glib."[23]

How closely Fitzgerald consulted his "General Plan" during the writing of *Tender Is the Night* is unclear. Not every detail listed in his notes appears in the book; Nicole does not lapse into "homicidal mania and tr[y] to kill men," nor is Dick as overtly political as the communist originally envisioned. On the other hand, his "plan" reveals that the novel's shifting points of view (from Rosemary to Dick to Nicole) were intentional and not, as critics would later presume, a byproduct of salvaging scenes from the Melarky drafts: "Part III is as much as possible seen through Nicole's eyes. All Dick's stories are *absolutely necessary*... [but] from now on he is [a] mystery man, at least to Nicole with her guessing at the mystery" (qtd. in *A Reader's Companion* 13). Once Fitzgerald decided to center his story on the marriage of Dick and Nicole, his plot structure came easily. The Melarky material provided his first nineteen chapters, with many of Francis's experiences transferred to the Rosemary introduced in the 1929 Kelly manuscript. The only significant restructuring occurred in Book II, where the causal explanations for Dick Diver's dissolution needed emphasizing. The effort Fitzgerald put into realizing this goal refutes claims by critics unfamiliar with the manuscripts that he was confused about why his protagonist fell from grace.

The novel's ambivalent reception, coupled with crushing financial problems, precluded Fitzgerald from attempting another novel for five years. By 1939, convinced that his observations on Hollywood could sustain a plot, he decided to further formalize his writing process to avoid the frustrations of 1925–34. As with *Tender Is the Night*, he produced a general plan, but whereas in 1932 his notes totaled sixteen pages, they now grew to include more than 200 of "character sketches, outlines, plot ideas, bits of dialogue, descriptions, biographical material about Irving Thalberg, background on Hollywood, and two Hollywood stories ('Last Kiss' [1949] and 'Director's Special' [published 1948 as 'Discard'])."[24] As with previous novels, he strove for a sense of structural proportion by dividing the book into units whose word totals would provide him with regular writing goals. Significantly, Fitzgerald for the first time produced a detailed plot outline to guarantee "a *constructed* novel like *Gatsby*, with passages of poetic prose where it fits the action, but no ruminations or sideshows like *Tender*. Everything must contribute to the dramatic movement" (*A Life in Letters* 467).

The 44,000 words completed before his death reveal that this outline was modular rather than linear. Instead of establishing a storyline he could complete from beginning to end, it charted discrete scenes to be congealed in a dramatic whole only after completing a first draft. Bruccoli suggests that screenwriting had intensified Fitzgerald's episodic mindset: "The screenwriter is writing for the camera, with the knowledge that the structure and pacing of the movie will be achieved through editing the film. Moreover, many screenwriting assignments are piecework, requiring the writer to work on individual scenes. It seems clear that Fitzgerald had become accustomed to thinking in episodes by 1939" (*Novelists* 40). Fitzgerald's declining health also affected his writing process; according to Frances Kroll Ring, his secretary during this period, exhaustion sometimes forced him to dictate dialogue.[25] The result, *The Last Tycoon*, was fragmentary, with many inconsistencies left unresolved at Fitzgerald's death. Most obvious was the problem posed by the use of a first-person narrator, Cecelia Brady, who – unlike Nick Carraway in *The Great Gatsby* – would not be present in many important scenes, especially those concerning Monroe Stahr's love affair with Kathleen Moore. Although Fitzgerald continually rewrote his first seventeen installments, he ignored larger unity questions, instead clumsily marking shifts in and out of the narrative "I" for his own benefit: "This is Cecelia taking up the narrative in person."[26] How he would have solved such transitional problems is, of course, unanswerable. Yet it is clear that doing so would have required him to reverse what Bruccoli calls his "composition by accretion" process in favor of a more sequential approach. As it stands, *The Last Tycoon* must be read as a collection of discrete fragments rather than an "incomplete" or interrupted narrative.

Major themes

Like most writers, Fitzgerald's thematic interests ran deeper than wider. Whether exploring the inevitability of loss and the thin line that separates failure from success, the quest for self-determination, the effects of class and money on morality, the attenuating values of the 1920s, or the dangers of dissolution and the struggle to maintain self-discipline, he rarely sought to reinvent himself but to patent his imprimatur. As he insists in "One Hundred False Starts," a good writer must repeat himself: "Otherwise, one would have to confess to having no individuality at all" (*Afternoon of an Author* 132).

Among these themes, the most pronounced is Fitzgerald's insistence that desire inevitably invites disappointment, for the gap between possibility and actuality is only rarely bridged in his world. His typical protagonist is distinguishable from the main characters of other 1920s fictions by his ambition. Both Leopold Bloom in Joyce's *Ulysses* and Frederic Henry in Hemingway's *A Farewell to Arms* (1929) – among others – react to events rather than initiate them. Amory Blaine, Jay Gatsby, Dexter Green, and Monroe Stahr, by contrast, are all driven to realize their dreams. While their aspirations differ (Amory and Stahr want to be great leaders, while Gatsby, Green, and many others conflate romantic fulfillment and upward mobility), their goals are, to quote *The Great Gatsby*, "commensurate with [their] capacity for wonder" (180). Moreover, they also believe in the gospel of prosperity, which assures them that their hard work will be rewarded. Characters like San Juan Chandler in "Presumption" (1925) commonly profess what the author in a 1936 interview called "an unshakable faith in one's star" (*In His Own Time* 296): "The inner sense of his own destiny which had never deserted him whispered that he was going to be a rich man."[27] The charm of these heroes is the naïveté of their conviction of success, which often begins in childhood. After Gatsby's murder, his father shows Nick Carraway a copy of *Hopalong Cassidy* in which the young dreamer had outlined the steps necessary to escape his lowly origins, including "No more smokeing [*sic*] or chewing" and "Read one improving book or magazine per week." As the proud parent insists, "Jimmy was bound to get ahead. He always had some resolves like this or something" (173).

Gatsby is among the handful of Fitzgerald characters who never doubt their resolve. Typically, protagonists must cede to failure and accept the illusoriness of their goals. In *This Side of Paradise* Amory is bewildered when academic, financial, and romantic setbacks undermine his "complete, unquestioned superiority," his certainty that he possesses the "qualities that made him see clearer than the great crowd of people, that made him decide more firmly and able to influence and follow his own will."[28] He spends much of the novel's second half seeking solace in alcohol and self-pity, unable to reconcile himself to his reduced circumstances until he discovers that their only compensation, paradoxically enough, is to transform the experience of loss into its own kind of pleasure. It is no accident that the words loss, lost and losing appear repeatedly throughout the narrative: "I've lost half my personality in a year," Amory complains when he feels that his "philosophy of success [has] tumbled down upon him" (100); a diversionary romance with the self-destructive Eleanor Savage causes him to lose "a further part of him that nothing could restore; and when he lost it he lost also the power of regretting it" (206). That Fitzgerald never clarifies what this "further part" is only reinforces the fact that loss has become its own goal, as a concluding epiphany insists: "I don't want to repeat my innocence," Amory decides. "I want the pleasure of losing it again" (239).

As *This Side of Paradise* suggests, few writers have ever obsessed over loss as intently as Fitzgerald. "I talk with the authority of failure," he insisted, distinguishing his melancholy temperament from Hemingway's blusterous "authority of success" (*Notebooks* 318). What can seem Fitzgerald's almost self-conscious pursuit of sorrow has led to charges of maundering defeatism, as when Hemingway in 1934 complained that because his rival "suffered so without knowing why" he was trapped in an "immature, misunderstood, whining for lost youth death-dance."[29] Even partisans concede that Fitzgerald's laments are sometimes overwrought – though what exactly constitutes an "appropriate" degree of sadness is debatable. When Arthur Mizener deems the oratorical ending of "Winter Dreams" deficient because "the discrepancy between [Dexter Green's] overwhelming grief and its occasion creates air of false rhetoric," he seems unwilling to accept that something as apparently frivolous as Dexter's adolescent infatuation with debutante Judy Jones can cause a formidable loss of innocence.[30] What such judgments fail to appreciate is that loss for Fitzgerald is not an indulgence but an index of heroism, for one's ability to accept its inevitability without succumbing to despair is for him the ultimate ethical challenge.

He states this point explicitly in *The Crack-Up* (1936), whose titular first entry defines the "philosophy [that he] fitted on to [his] early adult life":

> Life, ten years ago, was largely a personal matter. I must hold in balance the sense of the futility of effort and the sense of the necessity of struggle; the conviction of the inevitability of failure and still the determination to "succeed" – and, more than these, the contradiction between the dead hand of the past and the high intentions of the future. If I could do this through the common ills – domestic, professional, and personal – then the ego would continue as an arrow shot from nothingness to nothingness with such force that only gravity would bring it to earth at last.[31]

That Fitzgerald in 1936 deemed this mindset unsuitable for middle age does not diminish its importance to his characters, who maintain the struggle to "see that things are hopeless and yet [remain] determined to make them otherwise" (69). *The Beautiful and Damned* suggests one approach by invoking the poetic conceit of mutability, which insists that beauty's true source is not its immortal perfection but its impermanence. When Anthony and Gloria Patch visit Robert E. Lee's Arlington estate, Gloria objects to the restoration project that has transformed the old house into a tourist stop:

> Beautiful things grow to a certain height and then they fail and fade off, breathing out memories as they decay. And just as any period decays in our minds, the things of that period should decay too, and in that way they're preserved for a while in the few hearts like mine that react to them ... There's no beauty without poignancy and there's no poignancy without the feeling that it's going, men, names, books, houses – bound for dust – mortal –   (166–7)

Talk of poignancy contradicts *Beautiful*'s putative theme, the "Meaningless-ness of Life," whose nihilism, as many reviewers noted, was antithetical to the author's sensibility. What the passage reveals is how central for Fitzgerald memory is in coping with loss, for it catalyzes the elegiac instinct that his great-est characters share. At its simplest, the longing that remembrances feed is cathartic; it allows protagonists to memorialize what they have lost by articu-lating the anguish of its transience, effectively preserving it by "breathing out" its significance.

In *The Crack-Up* Fitzgerald prefaces the aforementioned paragraph by insist-ing on "the ability to hold two opposed ideas in the mind at the same time, and still retain the ability to function" – the essays' most quoted sentence (69). Meditating on the mutability that Gloria praises is his preferred method for exercising this ability. The aesthetic operates most memorably in *The Great Gatsby*'s final paragraph as Nick equates Gatsby's commitment to his unrealizable dream to the American spirit: "Gatsby believed in the green light, the orgastic future that year by year recedes before us. It eluded us then, but that's no matter – to-morrow we will run faster, stretch out our arms farther . . . And one fine morning – So we beat on, boats against the current, borne back ceaselessly into the past" (180). Such passages insert "us" in that "contradiction between the dead hand of the past and the high intentions of the future" that *The Crack-Up* discusses, insisting that actively engaging loss is how we "beat on . . . against the current" that attempts to wash away faith in human optimism.

The necessity of engaging loss is further demonstrated by those characters who *fail* to recognize its inevitability. These are characters usually associated with Fitzgerald's theory of "emotional bankruptcy," a term critics borrow from the title of his final Josephine Perry story. As Mizener explains, "The possibility of vitality's exhaustion led Fitzgerald gradually to think of vitality as if it were a fixed sum, like money in the bank. Against this account you drew until, piece by piece, the sum was spent and you found yourself emotionally bankrupt" (267). Failing to recognize that her emotional resources are finite, seventeen-year-old Josephine squanders them on a series of frivolous flirtations throughout the five stories in her series. (The other four are "First Blood," "A Nice Quiet Place," "A Woman with a Past," and "A Snobbish Story," all written 1930–1). "Emotional Bankruptcy" finds her shocked to discover that she no longer feels anything when kissed by the swains whom she mercilessly coquettes: "How strange," she decides upon petting with Martin Munn. "He's so attractive, but I didn't enjoy kissing him at all. For the first time in my life – even when it was a man I didn't especially care for – I had no feeling about him at all. I've often been bored afterward, but at the time it's always meant something." The consequence of regarding love as "a game played with technical mastery" becomes apparent when she meets her ideal man, the dashing Edward Dicer. Although attracted to the young soldier, Josephine finds herself incapable of bonding: "All the old things are true [she realized]. One cannot both spend and have. The love of her life had come by, and looking in her empty basket, she had found not a flower left for him – not one . . . 'Oh, what have I done to myself?' she wailed. 'What have I done?'" (*Short Stories* 550, 551, 560).

Again, some critics are reluctant to accept teenage romance as a sufficiently tragic context for so dramatic a motif. Yet Josephine's predicament is no different from Dick Diver's, even if his downfall seems more epic because Fitzgerald conceived *Tender Is the Night* as an epochal work. What neither Josephine nor Dick knows is how to accept loss. As Fitzgerald wrote to Edmund Wilson, he conceived Dr Diver as "an 'homme epuisé [*sic*],'" a "used-up man" whose emotional resilience is drained away. A superficial reading of the novel lays the blame for this condition on the strain of caring for a mentally disturbed wife. Yet Nicole is more a symptom of Dick's problem than the cause. He succumbs to dissolution because he has no mechanism for adapting to modernity, which has rendered his values irrelevant. Throughout the narrative, his work ethic is eroded by the temptations of expatriate leisure, his romantic idealism by the instant gratification of infatuation (of which Rosemary Hoyt is only one), and his intellectual eminence by the sycophantic fawning of his Riviera coterie. The reasons why he betrays these ideals are not only personal (his need to be admired) but historical, indicative of what Milton R. Stern calls the "post-war Western world confusion [that] undergoes disintegrations and refashionings in a morass of identity." Foremost among these "disintegrations" is World War I, whose bloodshed resulted in "the demise of the belief of the eighteenth and nineteenth century Western world in perfectibility" (*Cambridge Companion* 99, 104).

Among the values whose loss Fitzgerald characters must accept, none is more important than self-perfection, more often described as self-determinism in America for its insistence that identity is plastic and that success is limited only by lack of initiative. In his commercial stories Fitzgerald was apt to evoke the rags-to-riches myth associated with Horatio Alger, Jr. (1832–1899), some of whose interchangeable novels he had read during his childhood. Many critics regard "Presumption" as Fitzgerald's "anti-*Gatsby*" because its hero, San Juan Chandler, both rises through the business ranks *and* wins the rich girl who "can't live on air," becoming "a nobody no longer" by virtue of persistence and commitment (*Price* 193). "Your Way and Mine" – a 1926 story that Fitzgerald dismissed as "one of the lowsiest . . . I've ever written" (*As Ever* 87) – likewise celebrates this myth by dramatizing the entrepreneurial requisites of success: "For a temperament like Henry McComas', which insisted on running at a pace of its own, independence was an utter necessity. He must make his own rules, willy-nilly, even though he join the ranks of those many abject failures who have also tried" (*Price* 221).

Stories like "Presumption" and "Your Way and Mine" are often dismissed as minor works because they endorse rather than question the self-made man tradition. It is worth recognizing, however, that at least one major Fitzgerald effort also strove to celebrate the myth. In *The Last Tycoon* Monroe Stahr, having helmed a major Hollywood film studio since he was twenty-two, embodies the traits of great leadership: he is imaginative but not impractical, innovative but without alienating his audience, paternalistic rather than dictatorial with his employees. Another writer might have forced Stahr to question his principles through some crisis of hypocrisy, but Fitzgerald earnestly believed in the success story his hero represented: "In every possible way Stahr is a refutation of all the clichés about movie executives. Endowed with supreme intelligence and taste, he has elevated an art form without being an artist. There is no criticism of Stahr in the pages Fitzgerald wrote" (*Novelists* 7). "Tycoon" was not a pejorative term for Fitzgerald; in counting his hero among the last of them, he was acknowledging the passing of a tradition of heroic character that he admired. In Episode 3, Cecelia Brady invokes one of Fitzgerald's favorite motifs – flight – by describing Stahr as an Icarus figure: "He had flown up very high to see, on strong wings when he was young. And while he was up there he had looked on all the kingdoms, with the kind of eyes that can stare straight into the sun. Beating his wings tenaciously – finally frantically – and keeping on beating them he had stayed up there longer than most of us" (20). Yet the passage is a little misleading, for, unlike Icarus, what Fitzgerald imagined felling Stahr was not hubris but misfortunes of fate. Instead of delusions of grandeur, he suffers a heart condition that impedes his work. Similarly, the novel was to end with Stahr dying with two other Hollywood compatriots in an airplane crash, his body picked over by poor country children. Even after this strained plot twist, however, the mogul's innate nobility would prove influential: "The possessions which the children find," Fitzgerald wrote, would "symbolically determine their attitude toward the act of theft . . . The boy who finds Stahr's briefcase is the one who, after a week, saves and redeems [the other children] by going to a local judge and making a full confession" (*A Life in Letters* 411).

An interesting strand of the self-made man theme is characters' reliance on various models for their self-fashioning. Fitzgerald considered *This Side of Paradise* a "romance and reading list" (*Notebooks* 158) because it cites more than sixty titles and nearly one hundred writers whom Amory consults during his maturation. These resources range from childhood fare like *Dangerous Dan McGrew* to "'quest' books" like *None Other Gods, Sinister Street*, and *The Research Magnificent*, in which heroes "set off in life armed with the best weapons" for fulfilling their aristocratic nobility (115). The regime that Gatsby writes on the flyleaf of *Hopalong Cassidy* alludes to Benjamin Franklin's maxims for success in his *Autobiography* (1783–9), the founding text of the entrepreneurial tradition.

Other works employ Fitzgerald's "presidential motif," by which heroes' leadership qualities are compared with those of great American politicians. In *The Last Tycoon* screenwriter George Boxley equates Stahr with Abraham Lincoln:

He recognized that Stahr like Lincoln was a leader carrying on a long war on many fronts; almost single-handed he had moved pictures sharply forward through a decade, to a point where the content of the "A productions" was wider and richer than that of the stage. Stahr was an artist only as Mr. Lincoln was a general, perforce and as a layman.   (107)

Elsewhere, the parallels reinforce characters' *failure* to realize their potential. *Tender Is the Night* frames Dick Diver's rise and fall with references to Ulysses S. Grant's "Galena years," the period in the early 1860s when the general bided his time in unglamorous Illinois awaiting Lincoln's call to command the US Army: "The foregoing has the ring of a biography," Fitzgerald writes in Book II after outlining the doctor's background, "without the satisfaction of knowing that the hero, like Grant, lolling in his general store in Galena, is ready to be called to an intricate destiny" (118). That Dick's destiny is far from heroic is ironically underscored when, in the novel's final paragraph, Nicole learns that her now ex-husband resides in the undistinguished Finger Lakes region of New York, practicing general medicine instead of psychology: "Perhaps, so she liked to think, his career was biding its time, again like Grant's in Galena" (315).

The self-making theme also explains why romance is such a persistent plot point in Fitzgerald. Love for him is rarely a quest for companionship but, instead, a confirmation of the perfected identity. The women his beaux pursue are less important for who they are than for what they represent; they are the symbols and rewards of the hero's success. Readers who assume that *The Great Gatsby* is a love story fail to appreciate exactly why Gatsby seeks to win back Daisy after she is unhappily married to Tom Buchanan. As Nick recognizes, Gatsby needs Daisy to maintain his belief in his special destiny: "He talked a lot about the past," Nick writes, "and I gathered that he wanted to recover something, some idea of himself perhaps, that had gone into loving Daisy" (110). That idea is what Nick elsewhere describes as Gatsby's "Platonic conception of himself," one of the novel's famous phrases describing the ideal identity Gatsby invents when, as a teenager, he is mentored by the millionaire Dan Cody (98). Cody's largesse serves the same purpose as Daisy's affection: both confirm the "instinct toward future glory" that compels Gatsby to transform himself into a mysterious man of wealth, substantiating for him "the unreality of [his] reality" as a child of "shiftless and unsuccessful farm people." Because "his imagination never really accept[s his parents] as his parents at all" (98), he requires someone from the privileged world to which he aspires to confirm that "the vague contour of Jay Gatsby has fill[ed] out to the substantiality of a man" (101). One can argue that affirming this ideal self is the same solipsistic desire that Fitzgerald heroes like Basil Lee Duke must outgrow as they reconcile their expectations with reality. Yet the obvious sympathy that Nick expresses for Gatsby reflects Fitzgerald's respect for the poignancy of his "incorruptible dream" (154); even as Nick avers that "I disapproved of him from beginning to end," he cannot help but admire Gatsby's undiluted naïveté, his belief that "his dream was so close he could hardly fail to grasp it" (180).

Of course, love is not the only measure of self-making in Fitzgerald. Money is his second major currency of identity, and like loss, few writers have ever written as intently about it. As Hemingway demonstrated in "The Snows of Kilimanjaro" (1936), Fitzgerald's covetousness is easily caricatured to make him seem sycophantic:

> [Harry] remembered poor Scott Fitzgerald and his romantic awe of them and how he started a story once that began, "The rich are different from you and me." And how someone had said to Scott, Yes they have more money. But that was not humorous to Scott. He thought they were a special glamorous race and when he found they weren't it wrecked him just as much as anything that wrecked him.   (qtd. in *Epic Grandeur* 486)

Charges of sycophancy are hard to support if one actually reads "The Rich Boy" (1925), the story to which "Snows" alludes:

> Let me tell you about the very rich. They are different from you and me. They possess and enjoy early, and it does something to them, makes them soft where we are hard, and cynical where we are trustful, in a way that, unless you were born rich, it is very difficult to understand. They think, deep in their hearts, that they are better than we are because we had to discover the compensations and refuges of life for ourselves. Even when they enter deep into our world or sink below us, they still think that they are better than we are. They are different.   (*Short Stories* 318)

As Fitzgerald wrote to Ludlow Fowler, the college friend who inspired titular hero Anson Hunter, "The Rich Boy" offers an "unsparing but sympathetic" diagnosis of the paralytic effect of wealth (*Correspondence* 152). The plot follows Anson from Yale to World War I to a successful brokerage career, detailing his dissatisfactory romances with fiancée Paula Legendre and the impetuous Dolly Karger. What separates the rich from "you and me" is Anson's lack of affect, for his personal setbacks and thwarted love cause barely a ripple of remorse or regret. Not even the melodramatic revelation of Paula's death in childbirth phases him. As Fitzgerald suggests, privilege has snuffed the flame of ambition motivating less fortunate men: "[Anson's] aspirations were conventional enough . . . but they differed from the aspirations of the majority of young men in that there was no mist over them, none of that quality which is variously known as 'idealism' or 'illusion' . . . Most of our lives end as a compromise – it was as a compromise that his life began" (*Short Stories* 320). Instead, Anson's sense of superiority diminishes his initiative, leaving him to float through life "without the slightest sign of emotion" (*Short Stories* 348). In Mizener's view, "The Rich Boy" reveals that "like [Henry] James, Fitzgerald saw that one of the central moral problems in American life was raised in an acute form among the rich, in the possibilities of their life and – to give it no worse name – their insensitivity" (152).

Other works depict this insensitivity just as unsparingly – though not necessarily sympathetically. Conceived as a cautionary tale about the moral corrosions of wealth, *The Beautiful and Damned* often satirizes its main characters, thereby undermining Fitzgerald's inconsistent attempts to present them as tragic figures. Although Anthony Patch professes a desire to write, he never completes more than a handful of rejected articles and stories and eventually abandons a planned history of the Middle Ages. The reason why he is unproductive is that he considers labor beneath his class: "I want to know just why it's impossible for an American to be gracefully idle," he complains to Gloria. "I don't understand why people think that every young man ought to go down-town and work ten hours a day for the best twenty years of his life at dull, unimaginative work" (65). Fitzgerald's answer is a surprisingly conventional endorsement of the Protestant work ethic, with *Beautiful*'s plot insisting that idleness invites dissipation, as Anthony's and Gloria's sad descent into alcoholism and prodigality confirms. Sandwiched between endless episodes of their decay are comic vignettes that ridicule their sense of entitlement. In one scene Gloria, attempting to break into the movies, deigns to visit an employment agency, only to walk out after five minutes and promptly catch a cold from pacing Central Park hoping to "air the employment agency out of her walking suit" (370). Similarly, Anthony twice consents to an actual job, first selling bonds and later peddling a self-help scam called *Heart Talks*. After a few desultory customer calls, Anthony "conceive[s] the brilliant plan of selling the stock to the bartenders along Lexington Avenue. This occupied several hours, for it was necessary to take a few drinks in each place in order to get the proprietor in the proper frame of mind to talk business" (386–7). Such moments are hardly indicative of the "romantic awe" Hemingway complained about. Had Fitzgerald been as subservient to the rich as detractors have claimed, he would not have satirized their aversion to work so pungently.

The elite's fear of losing their superiority is the subject of "The Bridal Party" (1930), which explores the reactions of the rich to the October 1929 stockmarket crash that inaugurated the Great Depression. (The story was inspired by the Paris wedding of Powell Fowler, brother of the role model for "The Rich Boy".) Here revelers terrified by sudden financial uncertainties hurl themselves into festivities with forced fervor, hoping to forget their looming dread:

> These people were too weary to be exhilarated by any ordinary stimulant; for weeks they had drunk cocktails before meals like Americans, wines and brandies like Frenchmen, beer like Germans, whisky-and-soda like the English, and as they were no longer in the twenties, this preposterous *mélange*, that was like some gigantic cocktail in a nightmare, served only to make them temporarily less conscious. (*Short Stories* 565)

Against the backdrop of a romantic triangle, Fitzgerald employs one of his favorite plot twists, the reversal of fortune, to draw a contrast between protagonist Michael Curly and Hamilton Rutherford, the foil who is marrying his lost love, Caroline Dandy. While Michael inherits a fortune, Hamilton loses his. Had Fitzgerald written "The Bridal Party" in the early 1920s, the convenient see-sawing of rivals' prospects would seem contrived, yet here it is used to great effect to suggest the bewildering instability that compels the rich to Nero-like extremes of denial. Thanks to an unexpected job offer, Hamilton regains his financial footing in time to treat his guests to a lavish reception, yet Bruccoli overlooks the irony of this *deus ex machina* when he summarizes Fitzgerald's point as "American confidence had not been diminished by the Crash" (*Epic Grandeur* 343). Rather, Michael's realization that partygoers indulge themselves "at a different pace now, nervous as ticker tape" suggests a new anxiety about how long their party, both literally and figuratively, can last (*Short Stories* 576).

Despite his criticism of the rich, Fitzgerald did not romanticize the poor, not even during the 1930s' vogue for proletarian literature, in which several of his peers (John Dos Passos, Hemingway, John Steinbeck, Edmund Wilson) dabbled. Many of his young protagonists, such as Rudolph Miller in "Absolution," are ashamed of their working-class origins; whenever the collection box is passed in church, he pretends to be deep in prayer, "lest Jeanne Brady in the pew behind should take notice and suspect an acute family poverty" (*Short Stories* 268). The child even begs his priest for forgiveness for imagining he is not his parents' child (thereby anticipating Gatsby, of whom he was an early version). In "May Day" (1920) Gordon Sterrett hides his frayed shirtcuffs under his coatsleeves as he prepares to beg an Ivy League friend, Philip Dean, for a loan. Philip's response is blunt: "'You seem to be sort of bankrupt – morally and financially.'" To which Gordon can only respond, "'Don't they usually go together?'" (*Short Stories* 102). In Fitzgerald's world, they do indeed; his cure for poverty is, again, the entrepreneurialism of a Monroe Stahr. Consider how many Fitzgerald protagonists are aspiring businessmen: Dexter Green in "Winter Dreams" opens a chain of laundries; Jim Powell in "Dice, Brass Knuckles & Guitar" founds a "Jazz School" that is so successful that he moves "from his boarding-house to the Casino Hotel where he took a suite and had [his manservant] Hugo serve him his breakfast in bed" (*Short Stories* 248); most famously, Gatsby makes his fortune by embarking upon that most entrepreneurial of 1920s professions, organized crime. Not that initiative renders class boundaries obsolete. Fitzgerald heroes typically discover that their effort gains them only minimal access to Old Money respectability. "My God," Martin Van Vleck says in "Dice" while barring Powell from a party. "'Can't you see you're just a servant? Ronald [Harlan] here'd no more think of asking you to his party than he would his bootlegger'" (250). Tom Buchanan tells Gatsby much the same thing: "'I'll be damned if I see how you got within a mile of [Daisy] unless you brought the groceries to the back door'" (131). Even characters who do make it to this elite realm find acceptance rare. In *Tender Is the Night* Dick Diver must tolerate the condescension of Nicole's sister, Baby, who is convinced that he marries into the family for money: "She had looked Dick over with worldly eyes, she had measured him with the warped rule of an Anglophile and found him wanting . . . She could not see how he could be made into an aristocrat" (157).

One reason why money is an essential motif for Fitzgerald is that changing notions about its worth provided a powerful symbol by which to appraise the broader transformations in early twentieth-century mores. As the first decade to celebrate consumerism as a privilege of prosperity rather than a prodigal temptation, the 1920s experienced a profound shift in values as concrete measures gave way to increasingly abstract and arbitrary markers that had little demonstrable connection to the material world. Nowhere was the resulting instability better dramatized than in the rampant bond and stock speculation that precipitated the stockmarket disaster of October 1929. Fitzgerald's writing refers constantly to the ephemerality of modern finance because its volatility and irreality were perfect correlatives for the flux of a world in which one's "barber retired on a half million bet in the market" and the "head waiters who bowed me, or failed to bow me, to my table were far, far wealthier than I" (*Crack-Up* 31).

Fitzgerald recognized both the comedy and the tragedy of ambiguous valuation. Especially in his non-fiction he emphasized the absurdity of the era's belief in easy money, often at his own expense. His 1924 autobiographical *Saturday Evening Post* essay "How to Live on $36,000 a Year" lampoons Scott's and Zelda's already legendary financial misfortunes, including his irritation with a worthless $1,000 bond that he tries to redeem in tight times:

In all financial crises I dig it out and with it go hopefully to the bank, supposing that, as it never fails to pay the proper interest, it has at last assumed a tangible value. But as I have never been able to sell it, it has gradually acquired the sacredness of a family heirloom . . . It was once turned in at the Subway offices after I left it by accident on a car seat!   (*Afternoon of an Author* 89)

"How to Live" thus explores a common problem plaguing 1920s families who, thanks to expanding credit opportunities and installment-payment plans, lived beyond their means: the Fitzgeralds are cash poor. "The one thing it was impossible for us to do now was to pay cash," Scott admits when Zelda suggests that they shop at a grocery offering reduced prices for hard currency. "We had no cash to pay. We should rather have gone down on our hands and knees and thanked the butcher and grocer for letting us charge. An enormous economic fact became clear to me at that moment – the rarity of cash, the latitude of choice that cash allows" (*Afternoon of an Author* 95).

Elsewhere, Fitzgerald exaggerated the abstraction of economic values to farcical extremes. In "The Diamond as Big as the Ritz" (1922), millionaire Braddock Washington discovers a mountain-sized diamond that cannot be "valu[ed] by any regular computation . . . If it were offered for sale not only would the bottom fall out of the market, but also, if the value should vary with its size in the usual arithmetical progression, there would not be enough gold in the world to buy a tenth of it" (*Short Stories* 193). The inability of existing standards to measure the diamond's worth suggests the mind-boggling fortunes of the 1920s *nouveaux riches*. As was the case with much of this new wealth, Washington's exists only on paper, and maintaining it requires kidnapping anyone who visits his estate who might discover the diamond's secret. Despite its comedy, "Diamond" is not a satire of the entrepreneurial tradition that Fitzgerald lionizes in *The Great Gatsby* and *The Last Tycoon*. What is parodied here is not the rags-to-riches myth or even the ostentation of new money. Rather, Fitzgerald is questioning the *legitimacy* of any money not garnered through the only means he considered appropriate: hard work.

In tragic depictions of this theme, Fitzgerald was less ambiguous about the moral consequences of abstract finances. In *The Great Gatsby* Nick ambivalently enters the bond business, considering himself ethically distinct from the young men who flock uninvited to Gatsby's parties, "agonizingly aware of the easy money in their vicinity and convinced that it was theirs for a few words in the right key" (42). His sense of the industry's quasi-alchemical conjuring – it promises "to unfold the shining secrets that only Midas and Morgan and Maecenas knew" – are confirmed when Gatsby promises a business opportunity in return for reintroducing him to Daisy. Presumably, the favor involves the mysterious phone call received after Gatsby's death, during which someone named Slagle reports that a co-conspirator has been arrested for passing phoney bonds. "Babylon Revisited" (1931) likewise employs monetary metaphors for moral laxity. Returning to Paris after a sanitarium stay to reclaim his daughter, Honoria, Charlie Wales must determine why he and his late wife, Helen, succumbed to alcohol and marital discord. As he realizes, the boom corrupted his values, convincing him that work was unnecessary and that there was no consequence to squandering outrageous sums. Unable to comprehend the cost of his actions, Charlie locked Helen out of their home during a winter argument, causing her to catch pneumonia. The link between Charlie's irrational finances and Helen's subsequent death is explicit in the concluding scene, in which the now-recovering alcoholic lists himself among those whom the bull market tempted to sell their morals short:

> Again the memory of those days swept over him like a nightmare – the people they had met traveling; the people who couldn't add a row of figures or speak a coherent sentence . . . The men who locked their wives out in the snow, because the snow of twenty-nine wasn't real snow. If you didn't want it to be snow, you just paid some money.   (*Short Stories* 633)

Charlie Wales's challenge in rebuilding his life is the same one that several Fitzgerald protagonists must confront: how to maintain a standard of self-discipline in a world whose attenuating values encourage dissipation by glorifying excess and indulgence? As "Babylon Revisited" reveals, finances are only one arena in which the struggle to resist moral bankruptcy is waged. An equally self-destructive temptation is drinking, which, for obvious autobiographical reasons, is another central motif in Fitzgerald's fiction. Were the author writing today, he would probably depict alcoholism as a hereditary disease, recovery from which would first require rejecting the stigma traditionally associated with it. In the parlance of contemporary rehabilitation literature, he would portray it as an addiction one must learn to treat, not a character defect one must conquer. Yet Fitzgerald had little use for the medical redefinition of the ailment that was under way in the 1930s as his own addiction crippled his career. As his insistent use of the antiquated term *drunkard* suggests, liquor was a decisive moral test that determined the boundary between willpower and weakness. Central to this test are displays of resolve in which alcoholic characters must demonstrate their strength, often in ways that to modern readers seems like denial, such as Charlie's claim that he has cured his excess drinking by limiting himself to one whisky per day: "'I take that drink deliberately, so that the idea of alcohol won't get too big in my imagination,'" he insists to his brother- and sister-in-law. "'It's a sort of stunt I set myself. It keeps the matter in proportion'" (*Short Stories* 624).

Other characters profess a determination not to drink at all. Dr Forrest Janney in "Family in the Wind" (1932) sobers up after tornados devastate his Alabama hometown. Having "committed professional suicide by taking to cynicism and drink," Janney refuses to practice medicine, even declining to perform a life-saving operation on his nephew. Yet after the tornados strike, Janney discovers that "something purely professional that had nothing to do with human sensibilities had been set in motion inside him, and he was powerless to head it off." Despite his shaking hands, he tends to the wounded, including his nephew. His sense of duty reawakened, he decides not only to reopen his practice but to adopt a young girl, Helen Kilrain, orphaned by the storms. In the denouement he contemplates a drink, believing that "a man of forty-five is entitled to more artificial courage when he starts over again."[32] Like Charlie, however, he recognizes that such indulgence is incompatible with his new responsibilities as a father, and he declines, suggesting that all one needs to cure alcohol abuse is a sufficiently heroic motive.

In other cases characters that cannot maintain sobriety find their heroism in sparing others from their disability. In "A New Leaf" (1931) Dick Ragland, whose drinking has garnered him "the worst reputation of any American in Paris," leaps overboard during a transatlantic cruise when he realizes that he lacks the one quality that his fiancée Julia Ross desires in him: "the accumulated strength of having beaten your weakness" (*Short Stories* 645). Elsewhere still, Fitzgerald was guilty of sentimentalizing drinking by suggesting that the love of a good woman is a viable cure. In "Her Last Case" (1932) nurse Bette Weaver suffers a crisis of faith when her alcoholic patient, Ben Dragonet, shows little improvement. Tempted to abandon him, Bette must rededicate herself to her duty, even spurning her doctor-fiancé to devote herself to Ben.

John W. Crowley notes that, while Fitzgerald's fiction often takes a moralistic stance on drinking, in private he vigorously justified his own dipsomania, as in a 1930 letter to Zelda's physician, Dr Oscar Forel, who had dared to suggest that Zelda's recovery depended on Scott's sobriety:

> My vision of the world at its brightest is such that life without the use of amenities is impossible. I have lived hard and ruined the essential innocense [*sic*] in myself that could make it that possible [*sic*], and the fact that I have abused liquor is something to be paid for with suffering and death perhaps but not with renunciation . . . I cannot consider one pint of wine at the days [*sic*] end as anything but one of the rights of man. (*Correspondence* 243)

In Crowley's estimation Fitzgerald's boastful attitude about the baleful effects of his "amenities" is indicative of a modern tendency to glamorize alcoholism as a symptom of modernity:

> Fitzgerald was suspended between Victorian and modern understandings in a way that produced a peculiar ambivalence about drinking. "Drunkard" and "alcoholic" were not interchangeable terms; he perceived a subtle difference between them. Fitzgerald was repelled by "intemperance" at the same time that he was strangely attracted to "alcoholism"; whereas the former was stigmatized as a vice, the latter was distinguished (in both senses) as a sign of the modern.[33]

In actuality, these two attitudes were less contradictory than mutually reinforcing. Those alcoholic characters able to stop drinking do so because, in Charlie Wales's words, they recognize the need "to jump back a whole generation and trust in character again as the eternally valuable element" (*Short Stories* 619). The shame associated with intemperance is a vital regulator of character for them, for it provides a bulwark against the corruptions of modernity. Those who cannot control their drinking, by contrast, epitomize the emerging binge culture that celebrates self-wastage both as a compensation for modern uncertainty and as an embodiment of its consumer ethos of unrestrained satiation. What Fitzgerald said of his generation in "My Lost City" (written 1932; published 1945) is true of this segment of his *dramatis personae*: "Most of [them] drank too much – the more they were in tune to the times, the more they drank" (*Crack-Up* 30).

The point is demonstrated whenever characters appear to boast of their alcoholism or display it through self-conscious spectacles of self-destruction – just as some of Fitzgerald's peers (John Dos Passos, Edmund Wilson) suspected that he exaggerated his own inebriation to justify his boorish behavior. When Rosalind Connage spurns Amory Blaine in *This Side of Paradise*, he takes refuge in the "merciful coma" of a bender, breaking seltzer bottles at the Knickerbocker Bar, passing out at the Biltmore, and scuffling with waiters and fellow patrons at Shanley's. "'I wouldn't have missed it for anything,'" he brags to his roommate, Tom d'Invilliers. "'You ought to get beaten up just for the experience of it'" (207). Anthony Patch in *The Beautiful and Damned* likewise revels in drunken brawls, even losing a tooth after attacking producer Joseph Bloeckman for informing Gloria that, at twenty-nine, she is too old to be a movie star. In *The Great Gatsby* bystanders marvel at the damage done to a coupé when a drunk driver attempts to back out of Gatsby's drive. Much to the crowd's fascination, the driver is so intoxicated that he cannot comprehend that his car has lost a wheel:

"Back out," he suggested after a moment. "Put her in reverse."
"But the *wheel's* off!"
[The driver] hesitated.
"No harm in trying," he said.   (55)

"An Alcoholic Case" (1937) even includes a graphic moment of physical muti-
lation as a wounded veteran shocks his nurse while she is undressing him: "She
pulled up the undershirt; simultaneously he thrust the crimson-gray point of
the cigarette like a dagger against his heart. It crushed out against a copper
plate on his left rib about the size of a silver dollar, and he said 'ouch!' as a stray
spark fluttered down against his stomach" (*Stories* 442).

The fascination with self-destructive displays helps to clarify Fitzgerald's
most controversial depiction of alcoholism, *Tender Is the Night*. Critics have
long debated whether the role of drinking in Dick Diver's fall is sufficiently
dramatized. As Crowley explains, "On the one hand, the novel offers numerous reasons other than alcoholism for Dick's deterioration; on the other,
it subtly reveals the self-destructiveness of Dick's drinking. But most readers have been distracted from the evidence that Dick declines *because* he
drinks by the excuses Fitzgerald provides for the drinking" (75). Among those
excuses are other corruptions of modernity that the novel depicts, including
the legacy of World War I, the incestuous relationship between Nicole and
her father, and, most objectionably, the lesbian subculture Dick encounters
through Mary North Minghetti and Lady Caroline Sibly-Biers, whose rescue
from a Parisian jail is one of the doctor's few heroic moments in Book III.
While one can take Fitzgerald to task for portraying homosexuality as indicative of modernist confusion, it would have diminished *Tender's* epic breadth
had alcoholism been depicted as a personal battle rather than a "sign of the
modern." In the logic of his characterization, Dick's drinking must be symp-
tomatic of postwar confusion – otherwise, the novel is merely his tragedy, not
his era's.

To emphasize the equation of alcoholism and historical confusion, Fitzgerald
subtly links Dick's more outlandish drunken outbursts to the same instinct that
feeds his fatal flaw, his craving for "carnivals of affection" (27). Throughout
Book I persistent hints imply that Dick's charm is a theatrical façade designed
to arouse "fascinated and uncritical love." As Violet McKisco says upon meeting Rosemary Hoyt, "'We thought maybe you were in the plot . . . We're the
gallery'" (7–8). (In this part of the book, Dick's descent is foreshadowed by the
Divers' alcoholic friend Abe North, who is later beaten to death in an American
speakeasy). Once Dick can no longer sustain the illusion that he represents
"the exact furthermost evolution of a class," he indulges in belligerent, bizarre

behavior calculated to shock. Arrested in Rome for fighting with cabdrivers and cold-cocking a policeman, he is mistaken for another prisoner who murdered a child. As the court releases him, the misidentification inspires a mock confession: "'I want to explain to these people how I raped a five-year-old girl'" (235). When Nicole complains that his fondness for the word spic after a round of highballs "'isn't faintly like you,'" Dick replies, "'I'm not much like myself any more'" (260). And upon reuniting with Rosemary on the Riviera in 1929, he startles the now grown-up actress with a question: "'Did you hear I'd gone into a process of deterioration?'" (285). In each instance Dick melodramatically brags of his dissipation because making a spectacle of his decay is his only way of garnering the audience he once attracted through charm.

What links Fitzgerald's different themes is his concern with the self: what allows some people to triumph, what causes others to fail, and, most commonly in his work, what accounts for the poignancy that seemed the lingering effect of human interaction. Because individuals interested him much more than communities, he was a character-oriented author. Accordingly, drama for him lay in personality traits rather than plot machinations.

Major characters

"Begin with an individual, and before you know it you find that you have created a type," reads the opening sentence of "The Rich Boy." "Begin with a type, and you find that you have created – nothing" (*Short Stories* 317). Fitzgerald was defending himself against charges that his writing was populated with interchangeable stereotypes rather than substantive people, a defensiveness that was justified. Because he owed his initial celebrity to the popularity of a subcultural character with whom he became inexorably identified – the flapper – the public assumed that he was delineating a demographic group, not idiosyncratic psychologies. His persistent positioning of himself in the media as a generational spokesman likewise reinforced this presumption. Yet, however much he might expound upon flapper manners (as well as those of their male counterparts, alternately known as slickers, sheiks, and jimmies), his fictional treatment of them was not generic. His heroines respond differently to the dilemmas of sex, marriage, and self-determination, while the beaux courting them are far from uniform in their ambitions and class anxieties. Had Fitzgerald truly trafficked in types, the motives of major characters like Jay Gatsby and Nicole Diver would be transparent. As ongoing debates over their actions testify, this is far from the case. If his *dramatis personae* can be said to share any common trait, it is the one that makes parsing their behavior difficult: their moral ambiguity.

A good place to appreciate the variety of Fitzgerald's female characters is *This Side of Paradise*, which pits Amory Blaine against four distinct foils whose dilemmas would preoccupy the author throughout his career: Isabelle Borgé, Rosalind Connage, Eleanor Savage, and Clara Page. Among these, Rosalind captured original readers' attention because she was the book's most readily identifiable flapper (though the term does not appear in the narrative). Zelda herself endorsed the character, declaring, "I like girls like that" in a 1923 interview – an opinion no doubt influenced by her having partly inspired Rosalind. What intrigued commentators were the qualities Zelda applauded in modern women: "I like their courage, their recklessness and spendthriftness" (*In His Own Time* 259). As such quotations suggest, the flapper became a topic of cultural consternation because she rejected conventional notions of femininity, boasting of her nakedly opportunistic attitudes toward romance, materialism, and fun. With a winking tone of disapproval, *Paradise* plays up the supposed shock value of Rosalind's rebellious audacity, describing her as "unprincipled," "coarse," and "by no means a model character." Much of the charm of early Fitzgerald arises from his enthusiastic amelioration of such condemnable traits:

> If Rosalind could be spoiled the process would have been complete by this time, and as a matter of fact, her disposition is not all it should be; she wants what she wants when she wants it and she is prone to make every one around her pretty miserable when she doesn't get it – but in the true sense she is not spoiled. Her fresh enthusiasm, her will to grow and learn, her endless faith in the inexhaustibility of romance, her courage and fundamental honesty – these things are not spoiled.   (160)

Rosalind set the standard for such subsequent Fitzgerald flappers as Myra Harper in "Myra Meets His Family" (1920), Betty Medill in "The Camel's Back," Sally Carrol Happer in "The Ice Palace," and Ardita Farnam in "The Offshore Pirate" (1920), among others. (Although these stories are roughly contemporaneous with *Paradise*, the earliest version of the Rosalind chapter, entitled "The Débutante," appeared in the *Nassau Literary Review* in January 1917. *The Smart Set* republished it two years later.) In courting Rosalind, Amory discovers that the modern woman expects romance to be theatrical, with witty repartee and melodramatic professions of love. She also demands that suitors compete for female affection and prove that they will never bore their mates. Rosalind also shares with Amory's first girlfriend, Isabelle, another essential flapper trait: they believe that the truest register of a beau's romantic capacity is his kiss. "'I've kissed dozens of men,'" Rosalind "dreamily" confesses after she and Amory lock lips for the first time. "'I suppose I'll kiss dozens more'" (165).

From a post-1960s perspective, such professions can seem hopelessly quaint, if not cloying. In the context of the 1920s sexual revolution, however, the kiss evinced women's newfound freedom to "own" their sexuality – that is, to consider sex a pleasurable pursuit rather than a biological duty. "Sex" here is used rather broadly, for while Fitzgerald flappers often boast of their wanton kissing, their amorous experience rarely extends beyond the petting stage. Like the flapper, Fitzgerald became synonymous with petting, thanks to his then-provocative use of it as a title for a chapter describing the undergraduate parties where Amory dallies with "P.D.s" ("popular daughters"): "None of the Victorian mothers – and most of the mothers were Victorian – had any idea how casually their daughters were accustomed to be kissed . . . Amory found it rather fascinating to feel that any popular girl he met before eight he might quite possibly kiss before twelve" (61).

In celebrating the flapper's right to "kiss a man beautifully and romantically without any desire to be either his wife or mistress" – as Gloria in *The Beautiful and Damned* puts it – Fitzgerald proved relatively uninterested in dramatizing the double standard that encourages bolder expressions of female sexuality while reserving the right to judge their morality (113). Only fleetingly do his flappers worry about being labeled promiscuous. Shortly before meeting Amory, Isabelle learns that boys consider her a "speed," that is, an easy kisser. Later, while petting with Amory, she is irritated when his shirt stud gives her an "Old Nick," flapper slang for a hickey (or love bite), which will visibly corroborate that reputation (89–94). While Amory's inability to appreciate her fear incites an argument that leads to the couple's breakup, the issue never develops into a central thematic concern. The reason is suggested by the delight young characters take in taunting their elders with the threat of their sexuality, as when Rosalind's brother, Alec, suggests that his mother check the cellar if she wants to know where Rosalind has disappeared to during her debut (171). What *This Side of Paradise* demonstrated was that the flapper took her moral cues from her peers, not her parents, and thus felt little guilt over the (albeit introductory) sexual initiation that petting represented.

Even in later, more mature treatments of this character type, Fitzgerald invoked the stigma of reputation largely to discount its relevance to sexually self-possessed young women. In "First Blood" (1930) Josephine Perry announces her decision to abstain from petting: "'There's been too much talk around Chicago about me. A man certainly doesn't respect a girl he can kiss whenever he wants to, and I want to be respected by the man I'm going to marry some day'" (*Short Stories* 534). Yet the declaration is really an excuse to avoid kissing Travis de Coppet, a former beau whose romantic appeal has fizzled. Throughout her five-story sequence, Josephine does profess bewilderment over the circulating legends of her coquetry, but these moments are treated as a comic nuisance rather than the tragedy associated with similar ingénues like Henry James's Daisy Miller. As with most Fitzgerald flappers, Josephine's *paysage moralisé* involves outgrowing the flippancy of adolescent infatuations, not in overcoming the cultural prohibitions regulating women's sexual behavior.

One reason these characters are spared this conventional conflict is that for Fitzgerald it was subsumed within the larger drama of maturation. As his fiction demonstrates, the freedoms that flappers claimed rarely extended into the adult world, where women were still restricted to the self-sacrificing maternity and domesticity that the flapper's narcissism flouted. This lack of opportunity explains why Rosalind spurns Amory in favor of the wealthy dullard Dawson Ryder: without viable economic opportunities of her own, the choice she must make between financial security and romance brooks no debate. Readers often overlook the pathos of her predicament because of her flippant assessment of it; when Amory insists they can subsist on his modest advertising-agency salary, she replies, "'Darling, I don't even do my own hair, usually'" (180). Yet, Amory's other female foils substantiate Rosalind's point. Largely ignored by readers, Eleanor and Clara offer opposing glimpses of unmarried women's lives. The former, with whom Amory enjoys a summer romance, is outspoken about the limitations she faces: "'Oh, *why* am I a girl? . . . You can lope about and get bored and then lope somewhere else, and you can play around with girls without being involved in meshes of sentiment . . . and here I am with the brains to do everything, yet tied to the sinking ship of future matrimony'" (219). Eleanor protests against her fate with an aborted suicide attempt, the sobering aftermath of which costs her the last perk of adolescence, her theatrical penchant for posing.

Clara's story, meanwhile, suggests how a romantic regard for life is a luxury that unmarried women can ill afford. As a widowed mother of two, Amory's third cousin must exist outside of the "prosy morals of the husband-seeker, apart from the dull literature of feminine virtue" (131). She turns down Amory's marriage proposal because she knows his professions of love are made out of pity; he wants to save Clara from her near-impoverished existence. "'I'd never marry again,'" she tells him. "'I've got my two children and I want myself for them. I like you – I like all clever men, you more than any – but you know me well enough to know I'd never marry a clever man'" (137). Cleverness, she implies, brings little to the table beyond poetic facility, which is why she is amused rather than seduced by the flighty encomiums Amory improvises in her honor. Critics typically dismiss Eleanor and Clara as digressions, yet their episodes are necessary counterparts to Isabelle's and Rosalind's, for they demonstrate Fitzgerald's awareness that, however provocative, flapper mores were not necessarily revolutionary.

The winnowing freedoms of adulthood account for a personality trait that often baffles, if not outright irritates, readers: the willful childishness of Fitzgerald's women. Early in *The Beautiful and Damned*, Anthony is surprised to learn that Gloria is twenty-two, not eighteen as he presumed. To her, this is the highest of compliments: "'I'm going to start being [eighteen],'" she decides. "'I don't like being twenty-two. I hate it more than anything in the world.'" Intrigued by Gloria's brazen self-absorption, Anthony remarks, "'It's your world, isn't it?'" – to which she tellingly replies, "'As long as I'm – young'" (64, 66). In "The Offshore Pirate" Ardita Farnam throws temper tantrums, tells her disapproving uncle to "'shut up and go away,'" and even pelts the poor man with a lemon. As the narrator comments, "Though she was nineteen she gave the effect of a high-spirited precocious child" (*Short Stories* 78). In "Winter Dreams" Judy Jones is only eleven when Dexter Green first spies her on a Minnesota golf course; although he does not court her until years later, her behavior is no more mature. Several supporting characters even infantilize her: "'All she needs is to be turned up and spanked for six months and then married off to an old-fashioned cavalry captain,'" decides Dexter's golfing partner (*Short Stories* 222). This childishness demonstrates what Fitzgerald meant when he described the flapper as "playing along the danger line in an immature way" in a 1921 interview: juxtaposing the "baby" to the "vamp" allowed her to protest about women's lack of adult freedom by refusing to grow up (*In His Own Time* 244).

Fitzgerald did not wholeheartedly endorse flapper juvenility, however. Indeed, readers may be surprised to discover a rather troubling disciplinary strain that forces young women to bow to adult expectations. Both "The Camel's Back" and "The Jelly-Bean" (1920) end with their heroines tricked into marriages that abruptly halt their adolescent effrontery. In the former Perry Parkhurst sneaks into a party in a camel costume to spy on Betty Medill, whose secret engagement to Perry has not stopped her from living the debutante life. During a mock wedding Betty inadvertently signs the real wedding license Perry carries with him. Because the ceremony is officiated by a black waiter who turns out to be a real minister, the union is deemed legal. Only when Perry threatens to turn Betty over to the cabdriver occupying the camel costume's back half does the bride stop demanding an annulment and resign herself to her fate. Like Betty, Nancy Lamar in "The Jelly-Bean" prefers carousing to matrimony, but while drunk on corn liquor she weds Ogden Merritt, much to the chagrin of Jim Powell, the title character infatuated with her. "Nancy sobered up and rushed back into town, crying and frightened to death," reports Jim's friend Clark. "Claimed it'd all been a mistake . . . I don't guess Nancy cared a darn about him" (*Short Stories* 158). No annulment is granted here either; Nancy's ashamed father sends the couple to live with Ogden's family.

Elsewhere, the disciplining of flapper impudence takes place after the actual wedding. In "Gretchen's Forty Winks" (1924), harried Roger Halsey informs his party-loving wife that his advertising agency will fail without six weeks of shoring up new accounts. Rather than support Roger, Gretchen embarks on a flirtation with George Tompkins, who boasts of knowing the secret of balancing business and pleasure. "'She's a shortsighted little egg,'" Roger complains. "'She thinks it's going to be forever until I get started and she can have some new clothes. But it can't be helped . . . If a girl marries a young man for love she ought to be willing to make any sacrifice within reason, so long as her husband keeps going ahead.'"[34] In what seems a rather blatant metaphor for society's desire to narcoticize the flapper's selfish devotion to fun, Roger drugs Gretchen to send her to sleep. His plan saves both his company and his marriage, for upon waking, the wayward wife attributes her exhaustion to her whirlwind life and vows to settle down, a pledge reinforced by the news that George has suffered a nervous breakdown. "The Adjuster" (1925) is even more didactic; instead of a sleeping potion, the bored, childish wife, Luella Hemple, is tamed by the mysterious Dr Moon, who lectures her on her duties: "'It's your turn to be the center, to give others what was given to you for so long . . . You've got to cover up a few more troubles than you show, and be a little more patient than the average person, and do a little more instead of a little less than your share'" (*All the Sad Young Men* 190). While most critics view these stories as indicative of Fitzgerald's marital exasperation with Zelda, their severe attitude reflects the larger cultural urge to force flappers to assume adult obligations.

Fitzgerald's simultaneous adulation and admonition of the modern woman is most obvious in his two best-known female characters, Daisy Fay Buchanan in *The Great Gatsby* and Nicole Warren Diver in *Tender Is the Night*. Daisy's depiction is particularly responsible for the feminist objection that, as Judith Fetterley has written, Fitzgerald's golden girls are "scapegoats" for male disappointments because "even the poorest male gains something from a system in which all women are at some level his subjects."[35] The discrepancy between Gatsby's vision of Daisy as incarnating the "pap of life" and "incomparable milk of wonder" and Nick's more critical assessment of her "vast carelessness" makes it impossible to view her as a real person. Because we see Daisy only through male characters' eyes, we cannot access her feelings and motives; she is thus always either romanticized or scrutinized, yet never explained. In fact, what we see of her are mostly affectations. During Nick's first visit to the

Buchanans' East Egg estate, he is struck by Daisy's habit of murmuring, which, he has heard, is a gesture contrived "to make people lean toward her." He also notes the mellifluous nature of her voice, her penchant for baby talk, and the "thrilling scorn" of her laugh as she boasts of her cynicism and ennui, all of which lead Nick to recognize the "basic insincerity" of her self-presentation: "It made me uneasy, as though the whole evening had been a trick of some sort to exact a contributary emotion from me. I waited, and sure enough, in a moment she looked at me with an absolute smirk on her lovely face, as if she had asserted her membership in a rather distinguished secret society to which she and Tom belonged" (17). Daisy's unabashed materialism likewise does little to engender reader sympathy. A famous scene in which she cries "stormily" into the mountain of tailored shirts that Gatsby piles on his bed makes her seem superficial, while the later compliment she pays to her lover – "'You always look so cool . . . You resemble the advertisement of the man . . . You know the advertisement of the man'" – suggests that she is enamored with his image, not his earnestness (92, 119).

The narrative further indicts her for her lack of resolve when forced to choose between Tom and Gatsby: "'Oh, you want too much!'" she tells the latter. "'I did love him once – but I loved you too'" (132). By the time Daisy fails to accept responsibility for the death of Myrtle Wilson, whom she accidentally mows down while speeding away from the confrontation between Tom and Gatsby, her vilification seems complete. As Nick insists in the concluding chapter, she is no better than Tom, who feels little remorse for directing Myrtle's grieving husband, George, to wreak his homicidal revenge on Gatsby: "They were careless people, Tom and Daisy – they smashed up things and creatures and then retreated back into their money or their vast carelessness, or whatever it was that kept them together, and let other people clean up the mess they had made" (179).

While the narrative clearly positions Daisy as Gatsby's nemesis, readers should not overlook the tragedy of her own circumstance, which explains her inaction. For starters, she is an abused wife (she sports a bruised knuckle in her introductory scene) whose husband has a long history of infidelity (Myrtle is merely Tom's latest mistress). The passivity into which she retreats when Tom and Gatsby demand that she choose between them is indicative of what Ronald Berman has called her defining feature, her "psychological absence from events."[36] Despite her bubbly personality, Daisy is emotionally inert, capable only of reacting to situations instead of instigating them. Repeatedly, Fitzgerald associates her with stasis: we first see her reclining on a couch, "p-paralyzed by happiness," engaging Jordan Baker in "a bantering inconsequence . . . that was as cool as their white dresses and their impersonal eyes in the absence of all desire" (12). The tableau is repeated later in the confrontation scene, with both Daisy and Jordan positioned on the couch again "like silver idols weighing down their own white dresses against the singing breeze of the fans" (115). This decorative immobility symbolizes the compliant complaisance that upper-class women are expected to embody. Even after Myrtle's death, as Tom "intently" concocts a coverup to conceal Daisy's involvement in the accident (he does not know she was driving the car), she can only "once in a while ... [look] up at him and [nod] in agreement," her blank expression revealing her lack of agency. In a telling observation, Nick notices that the Buchanans "weren't happy . . . and yet they weren't unhappy either" (145). That seems an odd assessment for as dramatic a situation as vehicular manslaughter until one recognizes that Daisy's detachment is not an escape from responsibility but her natural state – she simply does not know how to be held accountable because nothing of consequence has ever been expected of her.

As further evidence of Daisy's incapacity for action, Berman points to a flashback description of her courtship with Tom, which begins while Gatsby is fighting in some of World War I's bloodiest battles: "All the time something within her was crying for a decision. She wanted her life shaped now, immediately – and the decision must be made by some force – of love, of money, of unquestioned practicality – that was close at hand. That force took shape in the middle of spring with the arrival of Tom Buchanan" (151). One senses that Daisy is looking for an outside force to reshape her life when Gatsby resurfaces in West Egg; otherwise, she would not consent so readily to adultery. Yet Gatsby's great mistake is assuming that Daisy has the willpower to decide what she wants. Unlike Tom, who bullies her into remaining in their marriage, he gives her the opportunity to choose, not realizing that his pleading results in the exact opposite of its desired effect: "With every word she was drawing further and further into herself . . . Her frightened eyes told that whatever intentions, whatever courage she had had, were definitely gone" (132–5). Ultimately, Daisy's plight, like the earlier flappers of "The Camel's Back" and "The Jelly-Bean," bespeaks Fitzgerald's belief that the freedoms that women of his generation were claiming were illusory. For all their insouciance and rebellion, they remained limited by social conceptions of femininity, something Daisy herself recognizes early on when she imagines her daughter's future: "I hope she'll be a fool – that's the best thing a girl can be in this world, a beautiful little fool" (17).

Two weeks after *The Great Gatsby* was published, Fitzgerald attributed its lackluster sales to his unsympathetic treatment of Daisy: "The book contains no important woman character and women controll [*sic*] the fiction market at present" (*Dear Scott/Dear Max* 101). Throughout the various incarnations that *Tender Is the Night* underwent over the next decade, one constant was the author's insistence that it be a "woman's book," with a strong female perspective to compensate for *Gatsby*'s "purely masculine interest" (*Letters* 247). The degree to which he succeeded remains a matter of debate. Although the narrative gives voice to Nicole Diver's internal thoughts and feelings (something denied to Daisy), some critics argue that the burden her psychological problems impose on her husband reduces her to a distinctly male symbol of feminine dependency. Thanks to Fitzgerald's editorializing narrative style, readers also encounter several dubious statements on gender differences that they may find objectionable, as during an early restaurant scene describing the interaction between Nicole, Rosemary Hoyt, and Mary North: "Their point of resemblance to each other and their differences from so many American women, lay in the fact that they were all happy to exist in a man's world – they preserved their individuality through men and not by opposition to them" (53).

Further complicating Nicole's depiction is the novel's persistent warfare motif, which portrays male/female interaction as a battle between the sexes. The point is voiced by one of Dick's patients, who attributes her excruciating eczema attacks to her rebellion against traditional femininity: "I'm sharing the fate of the women of my time who challenged men to battle" (184). Images of battle repeatedly intrude upon intimate moments, as when Dick's and Nicole's first kiss is interrupted by a burst of cannon fire (155). Dick even imagines the Divers' marital conflict in combat terms: "Though he thought [Nicole] was the most attractive creature he had ever seen, though he got from her everything he needed, he scented battle from afar, and subconsciously he had been hardening himself and arming himself, hour by hour" (100). The violence even becomes horrifically real when the Divers' entourage journeys to Paris. In the Gare St Lazare train station, Dick and Nicole, along with Rosemary, witness an acquaintance with "helmet-like hair" named Maria Wallis shoot a man. Although Fitzgerald never clarifies the motive, one presumes the victim is Wallis's lover. The incident marks a decisive moment in the romantic triangle between the Divers and Rosemary; shortly afterward, Dick acts upon Rosemary's naïve infatuation, thus making an irreparable breach in his relationship with Nicole (83–4).

Thanks to its ambivalent treatment of women, *Tender Is the Night* gives the impression that, as Rena Sanderson summarizes the conventional wisdom, "both male failure and social disorder are blamed on unruly female power" (*Cambridge Companion* 160). Yet, as with Daisy, readers should challenge themselves to recognize the narrative sympathy for Nicole. Having been doubly victimized by the men in her life – first by her father's incestuous advances and then by Dick's professional failure to maintain appropriate doctor/patient boundaries – she symbolizes the psychological damage wreaked by paternalism, which exploits young women under the guise of protecting them. Fitzgerald also accuses modern consumerism of a comparable exploitation. During a Parisian spree Nicole indulges in an afternoon of impulse shopping, splurging on everything from "a dozen bathing suits" to "a traveling chess set of gold and ivory." Unlike a courtesan's accoutrements, these purchases are not "professional equipment [or] insurance" but the conditioned behavior that capitalist economies must instill in women to maintain their market dominance:

> Nicole was the product of much ingenuity and toil. For her sake trains
> began their run at Chicago and traversed the round belly of the
> continent to California; chicle factories fumed and link belts grew link
> by link; men mixed toothpaste in vats and drew mouthwash out of
> copper hogsheads . . . She illustrated very simple principles, containing
> in herself her own doom, but illustrated them so accurately that there
> was grace in the procedure.   (54–5)

Although the theme of economic exploitation is not developed, Fitzgerald does suggest that one of the "very simple principles" dooming her is the illusion of choice that her buying power grants her. The poignancy of her portrait culminates in the final chapters as she resolves to leave her husband – not to be an independent woman, but to become the lover and eventual wife of Dick's truculent rival, Tommy Barban. Nicole wants to believe that a new relationship will revivify her youth: "She was enough ridden by the current youth worship, the moving pictures with their myriad faces of girl-children [like Rosemary], blandly represented as carrying on the work and wisdom of the world, to feel a jealousy of youth" (290–1). Her desire to be "worshipped again, to pretend to have a mystery" is quickly disappointed when Tommy points out the crooks around her eyes. Nevertheless, she does not reject his advances (or his insults, which continue). In many ways, the subsequent showdown between Dick and Tommy is the mirror opposite of Gatsby's and Tom's confrontation: here the husband indifferently relinquishes his wife to a belligerent lover. What the two scenes share, however, is their heroines' desire for their fates to be decided for them: "Nicole wanted Dick to take the initiative, but he seemed content to sit with his face half-shaved matching her hair half-washed" (310). The wish is instead satisfied by Tommy, who declares himself Nicole's "protector." Nicole's reliance on Tommy ("Everything Tommy said to her became part of her forever") contradicts her insistence that her affair has freed her from dependency: "New vistas appeared ahead, peopled with the faces of many men, none of whom she need obey or even love" (292). Because *Tender Is the Night*'s epilogue is devoted to Dick's evaporation into obscurity, we learn very little about Nicole's new life with Tommy. Yet one doubts whether she is freed from the obligation of feminine obedience. In her final dialogue, when she offers to escort a stumbling Dick from their breakup, Tommy, "pulling her down firmly," announces, "'No, you're not . . . Leave well enough alone'" (314).

Compared with his women characters, Fitzgerald's main male protagonists can seem downright staid, if not conservative. With the major exception of Jay Gatsby, they are generally less audacious and more conventional in their mores (though not necessarily less charismatic). The reason has to do with their narrative function: whether an endeavoring beau like Toby Moreland in "The Offshore Pirate" or a wastrel like Anthony Patch in *The Beautiful and Damned*, they are transitional figures who strive to carry forward past notions of integrity amid the temptations of the present. As they negotiate the moral upheavals of modernity, they speak the voice of caution, either by observing the excesses of twentieth-century life (Nick Carraway) or by succumbing to them (Dick Diver).

As the above distinctions suggest, Fitzgerald's heroes can be divided into two broad categories, aspirants and debauchees. A short list of the former would include the aforementioned Moreland, Dexter Green in "Winter Dreams," Jim Powell in "Dice, Brass Knuckles & Guitar," George O'Kelly in "'The Sensible Thing,'" San Juan Chandler in "Presumption," and, of course, Gatsby. Whereas the flapper resists maturity, these young men pursue the promised rewards of adulthood by flexing their ambitions. They also confront impediments that force them to question, if not relinquish, their dreams. As Amory Blaine in *This Side of Paradise* discovers, coming of age is not a matter of "going forward in a direct, determined line" (129). Indeed, after flunking out of Princeton, suffering through his family's financial setbacks, and losing his girlfriend Rosalind Connage, he spends the novel's second half mired in indirection, assuming and discarding radical new ideals like socialism in the hope of reawakening his sense of purpose: "There were days when Amory resented that life had changed from an even progress along a road stretching ever in sight . . . into a succession of quick, unrelated scenes . . . He felt that it would take all time, more than he could ever spare, to glue these strange cumbersome pictures into the scrap-book of his life" (215). Strikingly, *Paradise* ends without Amory resolving his predicament; he remains "a fish out of water in too many outworn systems" (256), disheartened to discover that experience has done little but reinforce his narcissism: "I know myself," reads the last line of the book, "but that is all – " (260).

A contemporaneous story, "Dalyrimple Goes Wrong" (1919), offers a more satirical commentary on the flustered ambition that Fitzgerald heroes often face. Bryan Dalyrimple becomes a burglar when, after returning triumphantly from World War I, he is relegated to a deadend job as a stockboy. The running joke is that Dalyrimple is as conscientious about theft as about work; as Fitzgerald suggests, criminal ambition arises from the same entrepreneurial instinct that the American Dream advocates (a point made more subtly in *The Great Gatsby* when Nick discovers that Gatsby is a frontman for gangster Meyer Wolfsheim). The equation of the businessman and criminal is made explicit when Dalyrimple's employer reveals that the veteran's unrewarding job was meant to test his resolve. Having observed him labor without complaint, the powers-that-be decide that he is an ideal candidate for the state senate. The opportunity inspires a reverie in which Dalyrimple lists all the ironic rules of success that his burglaries have taught him: "Cutting corners – cutting corners – common sense, that was the rule. No more foolish risks now unless necessity called – but it was being hard that counted – Never to let remorse or self-reproach lose him a night's sleep – let his life be a sword of courage – there was no payment – all that was drivel."[37] With his crimes going undetected, Dalyrimple is free to embark upon a new "scheme" (his backers' word) that will legitimately enrich him.

It is indicative of Fitzgerald's "doubleness" – his penchant for depicting both sides of an issue – that his aspirants' ambitions are often treated as sincerely as "Dalyrimple Goes Wrong" satirizes them. As previously noted, few moguls in American literature are depicted as earnestly as Monroe Stahr in *The Last Tycoon*; Stahr is a heroic figure because, as he puts it while explaining his studio's operations, "I'm the unity" (58). He alone understands the audience's fascination with movies, which he must leverage against the medium's duty to inspire rather than pander to public expectations. He also knows how to finesse the fragile egos of writers and actors. Most importantly, he never doubts or betrays his values; in the battle with Pat Brady over studio control that was to have constituted the latter half of the plot, Stahr was to be destroyed by an external rather than internal conflict: he would be "the self-made man whose destruction is brought about by the business organization that his talents and imagination have created. His studio has become so large and complex that he can no longer control its destiny. Instead, he is caught between the divisive forces that are fighting for domination."[38] While Gatsby does not realize his dream, it is important to remember that he never doubts it. Even after Tom reveals his gangster affiliations and Daisy accidentally kills Myrtle, Gatsby clings to his optimism: "'I suppose Daisy'll call, too,'" he "anxiously" tells Nick in their last conversation (154). Were he to die disillusioned, *Gatsby*'s poignancy would be severely muted.

In a similar vein, many of Fitzgerald's commercial stories wholeheartedly endorse entrepreneurial virtues. In "A Penny Spent" and "Not in the

Guidebook" (both 1925), young heroes embark on business enterprises that strike observers as foolishly risky; both the one-named Corcoran and Bill Driscoll succeed through a combination of verve and vision. "Hot and Cold Blood" (1923) and "A Change of Class" (1931) find Jim Mather and Philip Jadwin tempted to abandon their ethics to advance their own interests, only to learn through a sudden financial crisis the importance of self-sacrifice and service to others. "Two for a Cent" (1922) and "John Jackson's Arcady" (1924), meanwhile, are examples of what Bruccoli calls Fitzgerald's "roots-pilgrimage motif," in which protagonists (both uncharacteristically middle-aged men) overcome moral crises by journeying home to reconnect with their humble origins (*Price* 143). For readers who prefer their literature anguished and angst-ridden, such efforts may seem downright Rotarian in their unwavering faith in American business values. Yet they are historical reminders that in an age in which Sinclair Lewis's *Babbitt* (1922) skewered bourgeois aspiration, there remained a market for fiction about men honestly making their way in the world. Indeed, during Fitzgerald's lifetime, "John Jackson's Arcady" was one of his most widely read stories; in 1928 it was even adapted into a pamphlet for use in public-speaking competitions.

One might expect Fitzgerald to employ aspirants in these more commercial efforts and reserve his wastrels for darker plots. Yet his magazine fiction contains any number of Anthony Patches and Dick Divers, whose dissipation we have already discussed. In "Two Wrongs" (1930) producer Bill McChesney begins drinking heavily after producing two consecutive Broadway flops and emigrating to London; like Charlie Wales in "Babylon Revisited," he recognizes that his dissolution is a failure of character. "Six of One – " (1932) extends that indictment to an entire generation as two friends, Jack Schofield and Ed Barnes, place wagers over who have more resolve, working-class or wealthy boys. Not surprisingly, the less privileged youth prove greater successes, with the scions generally lacking drive. Ed, the poorer boys' advocate, assesses the detrimental effects of privilege:

> Schofield has seen his sons and their friends as samurai, as something shining and glorious and young, perhaps as something he had missed from his own youth. There was later a price to be paid by those boys, all too fulfilled, with the whole balance of their life pulled forward into their youth so that everything afterward would inevitably be anticlimax; these boys brought up as princes with none of the responsibilities of princes! (*Short Stories* 679)

And in "Financing Finnegan" (1938), an agent and editor bearing a striking resemblance to Harold Ober and Maxwell Perkins lend an impecunious writer so much money that their only hope of recovering it is to collect on his life insurance. The pair are relieved to think that the debt will finally be recouped when Finnegan is reported lost in a polar expedition. Their hopes are short-lived, however, for the author is rescued and immediately wires for yet another loan to book his passage home. The story suggests the shame Fitzgerald felt about imposing financially on Ober and Perkins. It also reveals his awareness that debtors like himself and Finnegan were not likely to reform.

Whether aspirants or debauchees, Fitzgerald's protagonists usually share several characteristics. Many are aspiring intellectuals, a trait that the author's detractors delighted in criticizing. *This Side of Paradise* makes reference to several strains of fashionable thought, with Amory Blaine at various points declaring himself a Keatsian Romantic, an art for art's sake aesthete, and a Nietzschean nihilist. In the final pages he even amuses a leading captain of industry, Mr Ferrenby, with his uninformed advocacy of socialism. References to philosophical schools come so fast and furiously that Amory's ponderousness can seem pretentious, which is why Edmund Wilson ungenerously dismissed Fitzgerald's alter ego as an "intellectual fake of the first order" (*Letters* 45) and *Paradise* for "not [being] *about* anything: its intellectual and moral content amounts to little more than a gesture – a gesture of indefinite revolt" (*In His Own Time* 405). The criticism did not dampen Fitzgerald's ambition to write a novel of ideas. Even more frequently than *Paradise, The Beautiful and Damned* references Nietzsche, whose denunciations of Christianity were popularized in America by *The Smart Set* co-editor H. L. Mencken. A central *Beautiful* chapter, "Symposium," finds the Patches' friend Maury Noble (based on *The Smart Set*'s other editor, George Jean Nathan) insisting that the Bible was written "to mock the credulity of man" (257–8). The passage was provocative enough for Perkins to recommend excising it, which Fitzgerald angrily refused to do (*Dear Scott/Dear Max* 45). (Indeed, he published it as a short story, "The Far-Seeing Skeptics," in *The Smart Set.*) Yet Maury's speech strikes most readers as extraneous, for it neither advances the plot nor develops the characters. In straining to lend a patina of intellectual justification to the Patches' dissolution, the interlude succeeds only in calling attention to its own gratuitousness.

Not until *Tender Is the Night* would Fitzgerald create a character whose philosophical affiliations were organic to the plot. Because Dick Diver is a psychologist, the abundant references to Freud are not only appropriate but thematically valuable, for they help to explain the doctor's downfall. Rather than show Dick discoursing on these theories, Fitzgerald reveals how he is subject to them. While Dick acknowledges that Nicole's initial attraction is a textbook example of Freudian "transference" (she projects her dependency on her father onto him), he fails to appreciate the dangers of his own "counter-transference" (his need to be admired by compliant girl-women), despite an explicit warning from his mentors (139). His susceptibility to this therapeutic risk is apparent as well in his treatment of other patients. As Dick consoles the eczema-plagued woman, he feels his desire to relieve her suffering "[going] out to her unreservedly, almost sexually. He wanted to gather her up in his arms, as he so often had Nicole, and cherish even her mistakes, so deeply were they part of her" (185). Shortly afterward, Dick receives a letter from the mother of another former patient that "accused him in no uncertain terms of having seduced her daughter" (187). Although he had indeed kissed this girl "in an idle, almost indulgent way," he refuses to ponder the reasons for his unprofessional behavior (186). It is not enough to dismiss Dick as a bad doctor; Fitzgerald is making a larger point. Theories and philosophies may explain human behavior, he implies, but controlling it is an entirely different matter.

These protagonists are also notable for their ambivalence toward sex. For all the talk of petting in Fitzgerald's fiction, his men remain curiously Victorian in their inhibitions, which surface in often odd ways. When Amory in *This Side of Paradise* is tempted by a promiscuous showgirl, he is chased from her apartment by an apparition that turns out to be none other than the Devil himself. Later, in a hotel room with another disreputable woman (this one picked up by Rosalind's brother, Alec), he is oppressed by an "aura, gossamer as a moonbeam, tainted as stale, weak wine ... a horror" that is relieved only by the appearance of his deceased mentor Monsignor Darcy, whose spirit is protecting him (108–9). More than one reviewer questioned how such priggishness could jibe with the novel's self-conscious impudence. Yet, as Bruccoli suggests, these scenes "dramatize Amory's sense of spiritual corruptibility, for, despite the novel's iconoclastic reputation, he is committed to moral and social order" (*Epic Grandeur* 145).

Sex is also a central motif in Dick Diver's dissolution. His attraction to Rosemary intensifies upon learning that the virginal actress was once caught *in flagrante delicto* on a train with a Yale undergraduate. True to his Freudian tendencies, Dick continuously imagines the scene of her seduction until his "repetition compulsion" becomes a voyeuristic substitute for his own unconsummated passion:

> Only the image of a third person, even a vanished one, entering into his relation with Rosemary was needed to throw him off his balance and send through him waves of pain, misery, desire, desperation. The vividly pictured hand on Rosemary's cheek, the quicker breath, the white excitement of the event viewed from outside, the inviolable secret warmth within. – Do you mind if I pull down the curtain?   (88)

When Dick and Rosemary do finally sleep together, he demands a full account of her sexual history, thereby ending their affair. His ambivalence to sex also affects his relationship with his wife. When Dick learns that Nicole is leaving him for Tommy, he mocks her recovery from incest with what may be the most brutal line in all of Fitzgerald: "'I never did go in for making love to dry loins'" (310).

Fitzgerald's heroes are also prone to severe self-doubt, which accounts for the often transparent vanity and showiness that can dampen reader sympathy for them. Typically, his protagonists must compete against rivals who exude the confidence they lack, thus forcing them to resort to bizarre methods of proving themselves. Gatsby creates baroque legends about his background when he discovers that brutish Tom Buchanan, who possesses none of his ambition, has the one thing Gatsby lacks: a pedigree. Dick Diver's intellectual aspirations seem weak and effeminate next to Tommy Barban's violent, animalistic life as a soldier of fortune, while the only obstacle to Monroe Stahr's goal of elevating the moviegoing public is the studio's profit-minded moneyman Pat Brady. Fifty-year-old Tom Squires in "At Your Age" (1929) discovers that his rival, Randy Campbell, has something that for a Fitzgerald swain is even more important than money or brute force: youth.

Compensating for their inferiority complexes frequently hastens these characters' downfall. Yet in at least one case, Fitzgerald explored how a young man might overcome his insecurities. The eight installments of his Basil Duke Lee series (1928–9) trace their hero's maturation through several formidable initiation experiences that reveal his weaknesses. Both "The Freshest Boy" and "He Thinks He's Wonderful" (both 1928) concern Basil's painful awareness of his conceitedness. In the former he decides to redress his faults rather than run away to Europe, and the story ends with him winning a modicum of respect from his schoolmates. In the latter his vanity is inflamed when he discovers that a circle of girls have voted him their favorite boy, and he offends the family of his current flame, Ermine Gilberte Labouisse "Minnie" Bibble, by talking about himself excessively. In "The Captured Shadow" he feels remorse for exposing a boy to mumps to prevent her sister from leaving for a vacation, while in "A Night at the Fair" (both 1928) he tries to protect a rival, Riply Buckner, from getting in trouble with his family, even though Riply has mocked his clothes. Basil's biggest challenge is developing a mature sense of romance; his flirtation with Minnie invites several social humiliations throughout "He Thinks He's Wonderful," "Forging Ahead," and "Basil and Cleopatra" (both 1929). Only in this last story does he outgrow his vision of Minnie as a symbol of attainment, and his newfound confidence protects him from further rejection: "He had made all his mistakes for this time."[39]

Major plots and motifs

As with his character types, Fitzgerald's storylines can seem deceptively narrow in range. Thanks to his association with the flapper, many assume that he wrote only about romance. Yet courtship is merely one of several preferred plots. As prevalent if not as prominent are stories of marriage, expatriation, and Hollywood. Additionally, Fitzgerald produced several didactic fictions in which the action illustrates a specific moral lesson. While these efforts rarely attract attention, they are interesting because they make explicit the moralistic strain that runs throughout his writing.

Courtship stories

According to Scott Donaldson, Fitzgerald's romances can be divided between those "depict[ing] the success, or seeming success, of the poor young man in wooing the rich girl" and those in which "the young man [is] rejected in his quest and [is] subsequently disappointed."[40] The distinction is convenient but too general, for it overlooks the oft-ignored fact that many of Fitzgerald's romances are told from the woman's point of view, not the man's. "The Ice Palace," "Myra Meets His Family," "The Popular Girl," the Josephine Perry stories, and even the Rosemary sections of *Tender Is the Night* are just a few examples. Even in the farcical efforts depicted in "Myra," in which a flapper's reputation as a "husband hunter" inspires a suitor to hatch a demeaning hoax to discourage her matrimonial aspirations, courtship allowed Fitzgerald to explore the previously discussed limits of female freedom. As an aging flapper, Myra seeks a companionate marriage, but Knowleton Whitney is convinced that she only wants his money, so he hires actors to scare her away by pretending that his family members are eccentric lunatics. Upon discovering the ruse, Myra turns the tables by duping Whitney into a sham wedding. As her final lines suggest ("He's getting off too easy – far too easy" [*Price* 32]), the victory does little to resolve the inequities between men and women. Whitney may be embarrassed, but he is free to move on, while Myra is reduced to returning to a debutante dating routine that she has long outgrown.

In Fitzgerald's male courtship stories, the plot typically involves confronting the social barriers that prevent the hero's self-realization. Among the successful romances, critics have shown a clear preference for what one reviewer called "gem[s] of romantic fooling" (*Critical Reception* 58) – that is, witty comedies such as "The Offshore Pirate" that depict love as a spectacular game in which the suitor concocts an elaborate ruse designed (unlike Whitney's) to win over his intended. "Fooling" here refers to a motif that Bruccoli calls Fitzgerald's "concealed identity gimmick," in which the swain's ruse centers upon an out-landish disguise (*Price* 126). In "The Offshore Pirate" Toby Moreland assumes the identity of the buccaneer-outlaw Curtis Carlyle to kidnap Ardita Farnam; in "The Camel's Back" Perry Parkhurst tricks Betty Medill by hiding in a dromedary costume. John M. Chestnut in "Rags Jones-Martin and the Pr-nce of W-les" (1924) pretends that he is wanted for murder and that his best friend, the heir to the English throne (actually a hired waiter), is spiriting him over the Canadian border, while in "The Unspeakable Egg" (also 1924), George Van Tyne passes himself off as an uncouth beachcomber to convince Fifi Marsden that he is not "too perfect" simply because "he remind[s] her of an advertisement for a new car" (*Price* 128). One may agree with Bruccoli's esti-mation of these efforts as "obvious reprise[s]" of "The Offshore Pirate" while still appreciating Fitzgerald's attraction to the disguise motif: it allowed him to dramatize the enterprising extremes to which men go to realize their destiny (*Epic Grandeur* 222). Fifi's reference to the car advertisement recalls Daisy's similar insistence that Gatsby "'resemble[s] the advertisement . . . You know the advertisement of the man – ,'" suggesting that these fantastic personae, like Gatsby's, are a mark of heroic resolve (125). Because self-determination is such an integral component of the American dream of self-making, dis-guises, no matter how absurd, reflect Fitzgerald's desire to believe that the only impediment to shaping the self is a lack of imagination and initiative.

Far less fondly regarded are sentimental takes on courtship such as "Love in the Night" (1925) and "Indecision" (1931), whose plots pivot upon coinci-dences, chance encounters, and reversals of fortune. In the former Val Rostoff must leave Cannes for the last two weeks of every April, overwhelmed by mem-ories of a young woman whose name he never knew. Predictably, that same timeframe is when she has been coming *to* the Riviera in the hope of reencoun-tering him. Their inevitable reunion occurs when Val finally decides to inquire about her at the American consulate, where for three years she has been leav-ing messages for him. In the latter story banker Tommy McLane has to leave Switzerland on urgent business, preventing him from apologizing after a jeal-ous spat with Rosemary Merriweather. When he discovers that she has booked passage on the very same train, he takes it as a sign that they are meant to be married. In "Presumption" San Juan Chandler is prevented from proposing to Noel Garneau when a protective aunt mistakes him for Noel's fiancé, Brooks Templeton, whom Noel has left because she loves San Juan. Only through a last-minute, fortuitous revelation of San Juan's real identity can the lovers reunite. What makes such resolutions feel artificial is the absence of the quality that makes the "identity gimmick" stories succeed: there is no assertion of destiny here. Rather than allow protagonists like Val, Tommy, and San Juan to realize their fate, Fitzgerald subjects them to authorial contrivances, effectively imposing plot outcomes rather than allowing resolutions to arise organically through character. The implication is that happy endings are a matter of happenstance rather than self-determination. Because critics tend to valorize literature that promotes self-empowerment, they are more apt to deem these twists of fate more formulaic than the disguise motif.

For most readers, the point of Fitzgerald's unsuccessful courtship stories is to question whether the object of the hero's quest – whether the girl herself, the ambition she represents, or both – is worthy of the imaginative effort that goes into its pursuit. Gatsby is the rare suitor who does not doubt his dream; far more common is the disillusionment Jim Powell suffers in "The Jelly-Bean" when Nancy Lamar's drunken marriage to Ogden Merritt extinguishes the "vague and romantic yearning" to be something other than a "corner loafer" that she briefly awakens in him (*Short Stories* 148). The problem with faulting Nancy for Jim's defeat is that it demonizes her for not living up to his expectations. A more productive avenue of analysis might explore how the theatricality that Fitzgerald associated with romance locks his men and women into gender roles that prevent them from achieving mature intimacy. The intransigency of these roles, not women's ethical failings, ultimately accounts for the swains' disillusionment.

This point is illustrated by "The Last of the Belles" (1929), the last of the "Tarleton trilogy" ("The Ice Palace" and "The Jelly-Bean" are the other entries) in which Fitzgerald fictionalized Zelda's Montgomery, Alabama, hometown. Conventional readings insist that the story traces the growing disillusionment of its narrator, Andy, with Southern womanhood, here represented by a predictably Zeldaesque heroine, Ailie Calhoun, whose romance with rough-and-tumble lieutenant Earl Schoen shocks Tarleton. According to Alice Hall Petry, Ailie has "never been worth the trouble of the narrator or of any other man, including Lt Horace Canby, who kill[s] himself after being rejected by a woman who essentially was simply a good imitation of a kind of figment of the Southern imagination" (158). Yet such a reading is overly harsh, for it denies both Ailie and Andy the self-awareness they attain as he struggles to understand why she violates her main criterion for courtship: "sincerity." While that word might not be the first choice to describe such a theatrical persona as the belle, it does suggests Ailie's desire to break free of the role's artifice to connect authentically with a man – something not likely to happen, given the melodrama in which suitors inveigle her. When Lt Canby dies in an aviation exercise after Ailie has spurned his advances – Fitzgerald never reveals whether it is an accident or suicide – her response may appear selfish, but it is also understandable: she sighs over her "involuntarily disastrous" effect on men (*Short Stories* 453).

Significantly, when pressed to explain her interest in Schoen, Ailie replies that he is simply more "'real,'" though Andy knows that Schoen really regards Ailie as another "jane" ripe for conquest (*Short Stories* 459).

When Andy returns to Tarleton ten years later, he discovers an Ailie who no longer embodies his own florid image of romance: "I saw she had a different line. The modulations of pride, the vocal hints that she knew the secrets of a brighter, finer ante-bellum day, were gone from her voice; there was no time for it now as it rambled on in the half-laughing, half-desperate banter of the newer South" (*Short Stories* 460). Again, most critics cite this passage as proof of Ailie's superficiality, yet such a reading fails to appreciate the poignancy of her inability to break away from her belle identity. Because Southern culture provides no other meaningful role, she must maintain the illusion that she is what men expect her to be. When Ailie announces her current engagement (her third since the war), Andy realizes that she will never marry him – and not because he is also guilty of idealizing her (which he admits) but because he alone doubts the image he projects upon her:

> She couldn't afford to let herself have doubts [about her identity]. I knew this because she had long ago stopped making any pretensions with me. This very naturalness, I realized, was because she didn't consider me a suitor. Beneath her mask of an instinctive thoroughbred she had always been on to herself, and she couldn't believe that anyone not taken in to the point of uncritical worship could really love her. That was what she called being "sincere"; she felt most security with men like Canby and Earl Schoen, who were incapable of passing judgments on the ostensibly aristocratic heart. (*Short Stories* 462)

Fitzgerald's beaux are guilty of romanticizing women, but the mature ones like Andy recognize that their idealization discourages "naturalness" in those relationships. As such, stories like "The Last of the Belles" critique courtship rituals even while glamorizing them; they reveal the tragedy behind the gamesmanship that Fitzgerald associated with love.

Marriage stories

Unlike these courtship tales, Fitzgerald's marriage stories cannot be divided into happy and tragic endings, for the former are simply too rare. In both *The Beautiful and Damned* and *Tender Is the Night*, contentious unions accelerate their protagonists' dissolution, while several stories ("Babylon Revisited," "The Rough Crossing," "The Swimmers," 1929) catalogue the emotional wreckage of jealousy, financial pressures, and gender roles. Not even commercial efforts such as "Gretchen's Forty Winks" and "The Adjuster" sugarcoat domestic discontent; rather, they overtly condemn immaturity, which Fitzgerald considered the major impediment to a stable union.

A major reason for marital disillusion is that Fitzgerald's couples discover that their vision of domesticity as "an ecstatic revel of emotion" (360) is unsustainable. As Gloria insists before marrying Anthony Patch, "What grubworms women are to crawl on their bellies through colorless marriages! Marriage was not created to be a background but to need one. Mine is going to be outstanding. It can't, shan't be the setting – it's going to be the performance, and the world shall be the scenery" (147). Although Gloria tries to stave off the drudgery of domesticity – both by refusing to do housework and by insisting that her husband address her as his "'permanent mistress'" (158) – she finds that routine dulls the drama of romance. The problem lies in the incompatible roles of jazz baby and wife that she simultaneously plays. As a vamp, she can taunt Anthony with her unattainability, yet, once his wife, her emotional needs become burdensome: "Gloria realized that Anthony had become capable of utter indifference toward her, a temporary indifference, more than half lethargic, but one from which she could no longer stir him by a whispered word, or a certain smile. There were days when her caresses affected him as a sort of suffocation" (277).

Lamentably, few critics sympathize with Gloria's predicament, dismissing her instead as a "slightly schizophrenic girl who moves between states of exaggerated excitement and melancholy pouting" and as "primarily concerned with getting her legs tanned."[41] Such judgments ignore the transformation she undergoes as Anthony falls apart. It is Gloria who assumes control of the Patches' dire finances, who pushes the legal effort to reinstate his inheritance, and who maintains the household. As Fitzgerald writes near the novel's end, "She was being bent by her environment into a grotesque similitude of a housewife. She who until three years before had never made coffee, prepared sometimes three meals a day . . . It is doubtful if she could have made it clear to anyone what it was she wanted, or indeed what there was to want" (424).

Gloria's domestication is reenacted in several mid-period efforts like "Hot and Cold Blood" and "The Adolescent Marriage" (1926). As in "Gretchen's Forty Winks" and "The Adjuster," these plots concern selfish brides forced to assume traditional wifely duties through a crisis involving their husbands' work or health. After 1930, their climactic reconciliations gave way to more pessimistic separations and divorce, with couples falling prey to jealousy and competition. In "Two Wrongs" Bill McChesney resents his wife Emmy's dedication to her dance career, which is on the rise as his own as a theater producer declines. When he contracts tuberculosis, Bill is hurt but not shocked by Emmy's decision not to forgo rehearsals to nurse him. In "What a Handsome Pair!" (1932) – a story inspired by Fitzgerald's bitterness toward Zelda's writing – Helen Van Beck and Stuart Oldhorne discover that their mutual interest in sports inspires rivalry rather than harmony. By contrast, Helen's cousin, Teddy, finds happiness with a former waitress who has no interest in his musical career. Teddy's concluding moral suggests how drastically marital travails altered Fitzgerald's image of marriage. If his courtship stories promote companionate partnerships, these late marriage tales bitterly insist that only traditional domestic roles ensure a happy home: "People tried to make marriages cooperative and they've ended by becoming competitive. Impossible situation. Smart men will get to fight shy of ornamental women. A man ought to marry somebody who'll be grateful" (*Short Stories* 696).

Expatriation stories

Like many of his literary contemporaries, Fitzgerald lived in France for much of the 1920s (May 1924 – December 1926, April – October 1928, March 1929 – September 1931). While there, he experienced the temptations of expatriation, whose advantageous exchange rate (nineteen francs to the dollar) made indulgence an affordable pastime. *Tender Is the Night* and several other works explore the dangers of profligacy, alcoholism, gender confusion, and promiscuity, which are key motifs in other period treatments of the American colony that thrived in postwar Europe, from Hemingway's *The Sun Also Rises* (1926) to Henry Miller's (1891–1980) *Tropic of Cancer* (1934) and Djuna Barnes's (1892–1982) *Nightwood* (1936). Whether residing in Paris or on the Riviera, Fitzgerald's literary generation seized upon foreign travel as a metaphor for historical displacement, making its immersion in an alien culture a symbol of modern alienation.

Unlike his contemporaries, Fitzgerald never immersed himself in Old World customs such as the bullfighting with which Hemingway became identified. As a result, his writing sometimes manifests a regrettable strain of xenophobia. His 1924 non-fiction essay "How to Live on Practically Nothing a Year" depicts French and Italian peoples as swindlers and extortionists, while sardonic descriptions of local cuisine ("a nameless piece of meat soaked in a lifeless gravy") abound (*Afternoon of an Author* 100). At least some of this nativism is exaggerated for satiric effect, suggesting that Fitzgerald was also parodying the expatriate presumption that Europe should cater to American tastes. "'The trouble with most Americans in France,'" a fellow expatriate observes in "Practically Nothing," "'is that they won't lead a real French life. They hang around the big hotels and exchange opinions fresh from the States'" – a judgment with which his companion concurs: "'I know . . . That's exactly what it said in the *New York Times* this morning'" (*Afternoon of an Author* 113). Elsewhere, Fitzgerald overtly condemned American chauvinism, referring in "The Adjuster" to "that enormous American class who wander over Europe every summer, sneering rather pathetically and wistfully at the customs and traditions and pastimes of other countries, because they have no customs or traditions or pastimes of their own" (*All the Sad Young Men* 142). His most famous essay, "Echoes of the Jazz Age" (1931), reiterates this assault, complaining that bourgeois affluence allowed too many provincial Americans access to a Europe whose history and tradition they lacked the sophistication to appreciate:

> It was evident that money and power were falling into the hands of people in comparison with whom the leader of a village Soviet would be a gold-mine of judgment and culture. There were citizens travelling in luxury in 1928 and 1929 who, in the distortion of their new condition, had the human value of Pekinese, bivalves, cretins, and goats. (*Crack-Up* 21)

These "cretins" compose the supporting cast of *Tender Is the Night*, which opens with Rosemary Hoyt meeting Albert and Violet McKisco, a gauche couple on the periphery of Dick and Nicole Diver's circle. Whether bickering – McKisco ends a seaside quarrel by rubbing his wife's face in the sand – or making a homosexual slur in the presence of a gay couple, the pair are ridiculed as "arriviste[s] who had not arrived" (33). Their pretensions are exposed when McKisco flippantly invokes the French tradition of the "code duello" during an argument with Tommy Barban and suddenly finds himself on the receiving end of a challenge. "'I've let myself be drawn into something I had no right to be,'" he admits (45), but that insight is promptly forgotten after the duelists' shots miss each other, and McKisco mistakes his luck for heroism. "'I did it pretty well, didn't I? I wasn't yellow,'" he boasts to Abe North, who reminds him of the source of his valor: "'You were pretty drunk'" (50).

Fitzgerald is contemptuous of these "fantastic Neanderthals" whose touristic view of Europe was "something, something vague, that you remembered from a very cheap novel" because they are oblivious to the moral risks of living abroad (*Crack-Up* 20). Like other expatriate writers, Fitzgerald dramatized these dangers through geographic symbolism, with different sites and locales embodying different aspects of his protagonists. In "Babylon Revisited" Charlie Wales is shocked to discover that post-crash Paris is no longer an expatriate province; former haunts such as the Ritz Bar and the Rue Blanche now either service "a local, colloquial French crowd," or, like the Café of Heaven and the Café of Hell, have become destinations on tourist itineraries. The relative absence of other Americans makes him realize how little contact with indigenous Paris he had during the boom years: "He had never eaten at a really cheap restaurant in Paris. Five-course dinner, four francs fifty, eighteen cents, wine included. For some odd reason he wished that he had . . . [H]e thought, 'I spoiled this city for myself'" (*Short Stories* 618). For those familiar with Parisian geography, the indirection that expatriation encourages is especially apparent during a taxicab ride in which Charlie twice crosses from the Right Bank to the Left Bank while revisiting old hangouts. This curiously circuitous route (which may have been the unintentional result of hasty editing) is indicative of Charlie's ambivalence toward his new sobriety and financial moderation. Throughout the story he shuttles back and forth between the sites of his dissolution and others associated with his conservative in-laws, Lincoln and Marion Peters, whose cramped quarters are located on the unfashionable Rue Palatine. Charlie's inability to relinquish his headier days becomes clear when, after a pair of past acquaintances, Duncan Schaeffer and Lorraine Quarrles, drunkenly barge into the Peters' apartment and ruin his chances of regaining his daughter from their care, he repairs to the Ritz Bar. A lesser writer would have his protagonist fall off the wagon, but Fitzgerald allows the story to end ambiguously, with the reader unsure whether Charlie returns to his old haunts to pay for his sins or to indulge his nostalgia.

As J. Gerald Kennedy has shown, *Tender Is the Night* likewise employs geographic symbolism to dramatize Dick Diver's dissolution, although in a far more fantastic manner: "Within the context of scenes that seem disconnected, hallucinatory, and even incoherent," Fitzgerald conveys "a palpable unreality of place [that] objectifies the confusion and ambivalence felt most keenly by Dick."[42] Whether on the Riviera or in Paris or Rome, Dick and his circle are increasingly detached from their environment, and they become incapable of comprehending the consequences of their actions. In what many critics consider the novel's most bizarre scene, Dick discovers a dead Afro-European in the very hotel bed where he and Rosemary plan to consummate their affair. The victim, Jules Peterson, had witnessed a bar-room fracas involving Abe North in which an innocent African-American was implicated; Peterson's murder is revenge for his aiding the police. To protect Rosemary's virginal reputation, Dick moves the body, but in hiding the bloodied bedding in his own bathroom, he causes Nicole to relapse by reminding her of her incestuous deflowering by her father. The "verbal inhumanity" of Nicole's breakdown exposes to Rosemary the secret behind the Divers' seemingly perfect marriage, marking the point where the fractures in their relationship become irreparable (112). The scene's conflux of sex, race, and violence is indicative of *Tender*'s insistence that expatriation encapsulates the menaces of modernity. By depicting characters bewildered by unfamiliar settings, the "American abroad" plot allowed Fitzgerald to examine how forces of change were cleaving the present from past traditions, leaving people with few sureties for coping with the upheaval.

Hollywood stories

Andrew Turnbull notes that during Fitzgerald's third and final attempt at Hollywood screenwriting from 1937 to 1940 "he kept a file of the plot-lines of pictures, just as he had once diagrammed scores of *Post* stories when he was learning to write for them."[43] His literary depictions of the film industry suggest that he was also familiar with the storylines of the nascent genre of Hollywood fiction, which ranged from farces such as Harry Leon Wilson's *Merton of the Movies* (1919) and P. G. Wodehouse's *Laughing Gas* (1936) to hardboiled moral exposés like Herbert McCroy's *They Shoot Horses, Don't They?* (1935) and Nathaniel West's *The Day of the Locust* (1939). Like these works, Fitzgerald was interested in the effect of celebrity on identity, the influence of movies on public morality, and, most importantly, the uncertain status of writers in a medium that, as antihero Pat Hobby proudly proclaims, "is no art . . . This is an industry."[44] His Hollywood stories (not all of which are set in the moviemaking capital) include a pair of 1927–8 stories inspired by his flirtation with actress Lois Moran ("Magnetism" and "Jacob's Ladder"), another by an embarrassing alcoholic incident during a Beverly Hills party ("Crazy Sunday," 1932), the seventeen Pat Hobby installments written for *Esquire*, a preparatory attempt at material that developed into *The Last Tycoon* ("Last Kiss," unpublished in his lifetime), and, of course, *Tycoon* itself, his most significant work about Hollywood. Additionally, major subplots in *The Beautiful and Damned* and *Tender Is the Night* involve the cinema.

"Jacob's Ladder" contains several plot motifs that would soon become staples of Hollywood fiction, including the Pygmalion-like relationship between talent scout Jacob Booth and the teenaged Jenny Delehanty, whom Jacob helps to transform into starlet Jenny Prince; the mentor's eventual loss of his discovery to a younger rival; and an attempted blackmail scheme that threatens to expose the star's lowly, working-class origins. Jenny's rise to renown further suggests both the facility and cynicism with which Hollywood was manufacturing fame in the 1920s. Although Jenny possesses little discernible talent, Jacob has only to beg a favor from director Billy Farrelly to make her a star; "in contempt for himself and his profession," Farrelly "engage[s] her for one of the three leads in his picture" (*Short Stories* 355). Similarly, George Hannaford in "Magnetism" has become "a moving-picture actor only through a series of accidents. . . . His first appearance in a studio was in the role of [an electrician] repairing a bank of Klieg lights" (*Stories* 224). Yet Jenny and George retain their self-possession. Jenny rejects Jacob's offers of marriage because he loves an image, not a person, a point dramatized with a daydream sequence: "His desire recreated her until she lost all vestiges of the old Jenny . . . He moldered her over into an image of love . . . creat[ing] it with this and that illusion from his youth, this and that sad old yearning, until she stood before him identical with her old self only by name" (*Short Stories* 364). At the story's end, Fitzgerald draws a parallel between Jacob's fantasy of Jenny as an ideal mate and the Hollywood invention of her screen persona when Jacob spots her name on a theater marquee: "Jenny Prince. 'Come and rest upon my loveliness,' it said. 'Fulfill your secret daydreams in wedding me for an hour'" (*Short Stories* 370).

Similarly, nearly every female character in "Magnetism" fantasizes about George Hannaford except for his philandering wife. Margaret Donovan attributes her unrequited infatuation (which inspires an abortive blackmail scheme) to the intimacy he projects: "'I loved you for years . . . You walked right up to [fans] and tore something aside as if it was in your way and began to know them'" (*Stories* 235). Although the star insists that his magnetism is "entirely imaginary," admirers refuse to doubt its authenticity. Even George's housekeeper falls under its sway. In the final paragraph she interprets a fleeting smile as "tearing a veil from between them, unconsciously promising her a possible admission to the thousand delights and wonders that only he knew and could command" (*Stories* 239).

Lest readers presume that Fitzgerald mocks fan identification as a female tendency, *Tender Is the Night* makes the audience's personal attachment to screen images a central part of Dick's fixation with Rosemary. The doctor may recognize that her movie *Daddy's Girl* exploits ingénue imagery by depicting "a father complex so apparent that Dick winced for all psychologists at the vicious sentimentality," yet he fails to appreciate how his sexual attraction to her arises from his belief that her innocence is authentic: she can embody "all the immaturity of the race," he decides, because she is "showing what [her fineness of character] took with a face that had not yet become mask-like" (69).

Fitzgerald's main concern with Hollywood was the same one preoccupying most literary depictions of the film industry: the lowly place of the writer in its hierarchy. For Joel Coles in "Crazy Sunday," the artist's outsider status becomes painfully apparent when the aspiring screenwriter performs a drunken imitation of a famous producer at a swanky tea: "As he finished he had the sickening realization that he had made a fool of himself . . . He felt [an] undercurrent of derision . . . It was the resentment of the professional toward the amateur, of the community toward the stranger, the thumbs-down of the clan" (*Stories* 407). Several Pat Hobby stories invert Joel's humiliation by depicting the industry's indifference toward writers from the perspective of the hack that *littérateurs* loved to hate. In "Teamed with Genius" (1940) Pat must collaborate with the vaunted English playwright René Wilcox, whose script Pat "improves" by inserting lingo guaranteed to appeal to a mass audience: "He substituted the word 'Scram!' for 'Get out of my sight!', he put 'Behind the eight-ball' instead of 'In trouble,' and replaced 'You'll be sorry' with the apt coinage 'Or else!'" (*Pat Hobby* 36). In "Pat Hobby's Secret" (1940) the "venerable script-stooge" hatches a plot to wheedle an ending from another playwright, this one "an Eastern snob" named R. Parke Woll. When Woll is accidentally killed in a scuffle, Pat forgets the ending, thereby foiling his hopes of profiting from the playwright's demise. The producer stymied by Pat's sudden amnesia voices Hollywood's frustration with wordsmiths: "He wished that writers could be dispensed with altogether. If only ideas could be plucked from the inexpensive air!" (*Pat Hobby* 60). In "Mightier Than the Sword" (1941) yet another highbrow literary type, E. Brunswick Hudson, walks out on a script, which Pat briefly inherits to rewrite until the producer replaces him with his secretary. When an indignant Hudson learns that his original plotline has been twisted to satisfy Hollywood formulae, Pat consoles him:

> "Authors get a tough break out here," Pat said sympathetically. "They never ought to come."
> "Who'd make up the stories – these feebs?"
> "Well anyhow, not authors," said Pat. "They don't want authors. They want writers – like me." (*Pat Hobby* 149)

Even though Pat Hobby was not, as some critics mistakenly suggest, an auto-biographical portrait, such passages suggest how the stories allowed Fitzgerald to vent his frustrations with Hollywood "feebs." Intriguingly, *The Last Tycoon* eschews Pat's hardboiled sarcasm to suggest what the industry might accomplish were it guided by artistic conscience. Monroe Stahr's sense of social responsibility is awakened when he encounters a black fisherman who refuses to allow his children to attend movies because "there's no profit" – meaning *moral* profit (93). Changing the man's mind becomes Stahr's aim: "He was prejudiced and wrong and he must be shown somehow, someway. A picture, many pictures, a decade of pictures, must be made to show him he was wrong" (96). The encounter inspires Stahr to reevaluate his production slate, discarding baleful projects and resuscitating others shelved for lack of commercial appeal. Unfortunately, Fitzgerald's notes make no mention of how the chieftain's idealism would contribute to the unfinished plot. While surviving outlines describe

Stahr's battle with partner Pat Brady for studio control, they feud over labor practices, not product. (Apropos of favorite Hollywood motifs, the conflict was to culminate in a mutual blackmail and murder attempts.) Nor is the fisherman mentioned again in the completed episodes; instead, the focus shifts to Stahr's attempts to curtail communist influence among his screenwriters, first by debating with and then by drunkenly brawling with an agitator named Brimmer.

Despite Fitzgerald's contention that Hollywood could not appreciate literary nuance, he was aware that writers' condescending attitude toward the medium reduced their influence. Two central *Last Tycoon* scenes involve Stahr's efforts to convince novelist George Boxley (based on *Doors of Perception* author Aldous Huxley) that the medium can accomplish more than "wearing strained facial expressions and talking in incredible and unnatural dialogue" (32). In the first episode Stahr improvises a scenario whose elements – a pretty stenographer and a pair of black gloves she denies owning – hook Boxley's interest against his will, demonstrating how the mystery of a plot is the necessary ingredient for engaging an audience. Later, when Boxley threatens to quit the studio because the "condition" of "mass production" limits his creativity, Stahr delivers a stern monologue on the role that movies serve in popular culture: "'There's always some lousy condition . . . [Ours] is that we have to take people's own favorite folklore and dress it up and give it back to them. Anything beyond that is sugar'" (106–7).

Once Boxley recognizes his role in the process – to provide that sugar – he becomes a productive member of Stahr's team. The chieftain's ability to motivate his employees is a testament to his leadership style; as Fitzgerald insists in describing Boxley's conversion, "Stahr had recreated the proper atmosphere – never consenting to be a driver of the driven, but feeling like and acting like and sometimes even looking like a small boy getting up a show" (108). Yet other episodes reveal the manipulative nature of this style. In his debate with Brimmer, Stahr bluntly admits why writers are marginal figures: "'Writers are children . . . They are not equipped for authority. There is no substitute for will. Sometimes you have to fake will when you don't feel it at all'" (121–2). While most Hollywood fiction depicts writers as hapless victims of sharkish chieftains, *The Last Tycoon* is unique for its dimensioned portrayal of a studio boss who, while aspiring to great art, understands the pragmatic machinations necessary to manage the business end of moviemaking.

Didactic stories

Fitzgerald also employed a plot form that garners little literary respect: the story that "subordinates the entertainment value of the story to its message."[45]

However satirically absurd the violent premises of "The Four Fists" (1920) and "The Pusher-in-the-Face" (1925), they are earnest attempts to convey morally salubrious lessons. The first dramatizes the benefits of (literally) "taking it on the chin" as Samuel Meredith's ethical sensibility is strengthened by four consecutive punches to the face. The second reverses the scenario with a metaphorical parable about self-assertion in which Charles David Stuart must overcome the meekness impeding his career by shoving irritating people. When one of his victims turns out to be a wanted criminal, Stuart is recognized as a hero. Other stories preach against materialism, as in the supernatural "The Cut-Glass Bowl" (1920), in which the titular object visits tragedy on Evelyn Piper's family, or financial irresponsibility, as in "The Rubber Check" (1932), in which Val Schuyler must suffer the consequences of overdrawing his bank account. Fitzgerald's audience often held these efforts in higher esteem than he did; when in May 1920 Princeton president John Grier Hibben objected to *This Side of Paradise*'s depiction of Princeton as a pampered country club, he made a special point of commending "The Four Fists" for "present[ing] a philosophy of life which I wish every young man of our country would feel and appreciate . . . I hope [its philosophy] may be further developed in your writings and prove a help and inspiration to men who may not be aware of the real power concealed within them" (qtd. in *Before Gatsby* 43).

Mode and genre

That Fitzgerald's works are often categorized within opposing literary traditions testifies to the diversity of his talent. While frequently labeled a Romantic owing to his affinities with his favorite poet, John Keats (1795–1821), he was nevertheless a member of the modernist generation, which dismissed the early nineteenth-century Romantics' dreamy, pastoral idealism as irrelevant to a twentieth century rife with war and change. When not negotiating those competing loyalties, Fitzgerald forayed into at least two other modes, realism and naturalism. Engaging these different traditions also allowed him to practice a number of their genres, from the *Bildungsroman* or coming-of-age story (a Romantic invention) to the comedy of manners (which, while predating realism, became associated with it). Additionally, he employed various techniques that emerged from these modes, whether the stream of consciousness and poetic dissociation of modernism or naturalism's ironic tone.

Lionel Trilling has identified Fitzgerald's most prominent Romantic trait: "He was perhaps the last notable writer to affirm the Romantic fantasy . . . of personal ambition or heroism, of life committed to, or thrown away for, some ideal of self."[46] Whether in *This Side of Paradise* or in *The Great Gatsby*, the hero's quest to perfect his identity recalls Romantic novels and poems such as Johann Wolfgang von Goethe's (1749–1832) *Wilhelm Meister's Apprenticeship* (1794–6) and Lord Byron's (1788–1824) *Childe Harold's Pilgrimage* (1812–18), narratives in which young men journey into the world seeking self-perfection through higher knowledge. Key to realizing this goal is the imagination, which Romantics revered as a conduit to divinity (as opposed to the reason, advocated by eighteenth-century Neoclassicists). Rather than accept the inherited reality of the external world, Romantics insisted that truth is best apprehended through what Amory Blaine calls "consuming introspection" (241). This is why Amory, Dick Diver, and other Fitzgerald heroes are prone to swells of emotion: their lyrical inquiry into their feelings is their learning process. This is not to say, of course, that their focus is wholly inward. Fitzgerald's use of the "golden girl" as a symbol of attainment also evokes the Romantic tradition of such "dark lady" poems as Keats's "La Belle Dame Sans Merci" (1820), whose literal translation ("The Beautiful Lady Without Mercy") was a provisional title for *The Beautiful and Damned.* In such works the protagonist is seduced by a vision of feminine beauty whose evanescence prostrates him with sorrow. One need only compare Dexter Green's closing oration in "Winter Dreams" to Keats's poem to appreciate how attached Fitzgerald was to this motif. In other cases he emulated the Romantic convention of the sylvan dream, in which nature, not a woman, hints at beatific truths that elude human comprehension. The title and epigraph of *Tender Is the Night* came from one such poem, Keats's "Ode to a Nightingale" (1820). Maxwell Perkins feared that the phrase was too abstract to sell the novel, but, as Bruccoli recognizes, because "Keats's poem expresses an attempt to flee painful reality and the consequent return to despair," it captures perfectly "the mood of disenchantment that pervades Fitzgerald's romance" (*Epic Grandeur* 402).

The painful gap between the real and ideal suggests the other major legacy of Romanticism: Fitzgerald's fixation with loss. We have seen how his heroes (save for Gatsby) discover that with aspiration comes disenchantment. Amory goes so far as to suggest that disillusionment is striving's compensation: "I'm romantic," he twice declares when first Rosalind and then Eleanor accuse him of sentimentalism. "A sentimental person thinks things will last – a romantic person hopes against hope that they won't" (166; see also 212). Romantics coveted loss because they believed that it taught the humbling lesson of human limitations. In a typical Romantic narrative – one thinks of William Wordsworth's (1770–1850) "Lines Composed a Few Miles Above Tintern Abbey" (1798) and "Ode: Intimations of Immortality" (1807) – the "I" attains a glimpse of transcendent beauty only to return to a reality that is incompatible with sublimity, resulting in a melancholy but earned appreciation of the circumscribed powers of imagination. This pattern is most visible in Fitzgerald's 1930s non-fiction, in which he dwells on his and his era's failures. Sometimes the disappointments he recounts can seem jejune, as when in *The Crack-Up*'s "Pasting It Together" (1936) he recalls "the junk heap of the shoulder pads worn for one day on the Princeton freshman football field and the overseas cap never worn overseas" (84), or when in "Early Success" (1937) he remembers how what was supposed to be a triumphant return to Princeton during *This Side of Paradise*'s glory days turned into such a debacle that "on that day in 1920 most of the joy went out of my success" (89). What such setbacks are meant to demonstrate is how incommensurate with Fitzgerald's early optimistic yearning the world proved. Dwelling on disappointment, he intensifies these emotions until they explode in cathartic climaxes: "All is lost save memory," he declares in "My Lost City," which laments the passing of New York's boom years. "For the moment I can only cry out that I have lost my splendid mirage. Come back, come back, O glittering and white!" (33). Although he did not employ the apostrophe ("O") as routinely as Romantic poets, his "crying out" is indicative of their exclamatory manner, which aimed to console by demonstrating the imagination's ability to elegize loss in emotionally affective ways. This is what we mean by loss being its own compensation for a Romantic: melancholy catalyzes the aesthetic instinct, which, by striving to communicate the pain of loss, effectively overcomes it by culminating in tangible art.

Fitzgerald's Romantic influences are also apparent from the various genres he employed. Critics disagree over whether *This Side of Paradise* can be labeled a true *Bildungsroman* – mainly because, unlike the standard "novel of development" that *Wilhelm Meister* established, it does not end with its hero becoming a fully mature adult. Nevertheless, Amory's romantic and financial ups and downs are typical of the coming-of-age dilemmas with which Romantic protagonists struggle, as are his moodiness and indirection. Because "Basil and Cleopatra" ends more definitively, with Basil Duke Lee breaking his dependency on popular girls like Minnie Bibble, his story cycle offers a more traditional example of the genre. As Jackson R. Bryer and John Kuehl note, readers can chart Basil's gradual maturation within his nine stories:

> Though he contains the seeds of failure, Basil emerges triumphant . . .
> This pattern [of growth] for the sequence as a whole is reflected in many
> of the individual stories. Beginning in "That Kind of Party" [first
> published posthumously in 1951] and continuing through such others
> as "The Scandal Detectives" [1928], "He Thinks He's Wonderful," and
> "The Perfect Life" [1929], Basil does superficially awful things or loses a
> girl but in the end is wiser or with an even better girl or both. (*Basil
> and Josephine* 22)

Another Romantic genre that Fitzgerald attempted may surprise readers, for his name is not usually associated with supernatural fiction. Yet the Romantic insistence that visions, dreams, and even hallucinations manifest phantas-magoric realities that rationality cannot comprehend appealed to Fitzgerald's sense of the fantastic. Although it satirizes 1920s materialism, "The Diamond as Big as the Ritz" owes much to Samuel Taylor Coleridge's (1772–1834) "Kubla Khan" (1816), particularly in its description of the "exquisite château" that Braddock Washington builds on his mountain-sized diamond in the Rockies. The estate's "many towers, the slender tracery of the sloping parapets, the chis-eled wonder of a thousand yellow windows with their oblongs and hectagons and triangles of golden light, the shattered softness of the interesting planes of star-shine and blue shade" all evoke Coleridge's "stately pleasure dome," whose majesty is both awesome and horrific (*Short Stories* 188). Fitzgerald also employed a favorite supernatural device, the *doppelgänger* or "double," in which a character is haunted by a ghostly counterpart, as in Edgar Allan Poe's (1809–1849) "William Wilson" (1839). In "A Short Trip Home" (1927), Joe Jelke attempts to save Ellen Baker from a mysterious figure, Joe Varland, who turns out to be a ghost preying on young women.

"One Trip Abroad" (1930) is a rare example of a supernatural expatria-tion story. As Nelson and Nicole Kelly wander through Europe, they repeat-edly encounter a dissipated couple whose "flabbiness" and "unwholesomeness" epitomize Ugly Americanism. Only after the Kellys' marriage crumbles do they realize that the other couple was them. Not all of Fitzgerald's supernatural stories are so dark. "The Curious Case of Benjamin Button" (1922) recounts the biography of a man born into the body of a seventy-year-old who grows younger rather than older. As Lawrence Buell suggests, what links these fantas-tic tales is Fitzgerald's insistence that "dreams of a metamorphosed reality are emotional and social necessities which we cannot help but indulge, and that they are in another sense insubstantial, ludicrous, pathetic."[47]

Fitzgerald's Romanticism was atypical of his time, for such leading liter-ary peers as T. S. Eliot and Ezra Pound had made the mode unfashionable by attacking it as excessively emotional and escapist. The modernist aesthetic they defined insisted on depersonalizing art with radically experimental styles, an approach that might not seem compatible with such an insistently auto-biographical writer as Fitzgerald. Nevertheless, he borrowed techniques from Eliot's *The Waste Land* and Joyce's *Ulysses*, not necessarily because he was inspired by Pound's injunction to "Make it new!" but because he shared the modernist conviction that his generation was charged with formulating a belief system to replace traditions that modernity had rendered obsolete. The mission is explicitly defined at the end of *This Side of Paradise* as Amory walks through the Princeton campus:

> As an endless dream [the University] went on; the spirit of the past
> brooding over a new generation, the chosen youth from the muddled,
> unchastened world, still fed romantically on the mistakes and
> half-forgotten dreams of dead statesmen and poets. Here was a new
> generation . . . destined finally to go out into that dirty gray turmoil to
> follow love and pride; a new generation dedicated more than the last to
> the fear of poverty and the worship of success; grown up to find all Gods
> dead, all wars fought, all faiths in man shaken.   (260)

"All wars fought" alludes to the catastrophic event that this literary generation considered the *sine qua non* of modernity: World War I. Much like Pound's denunciation of the 1914–18 conflagration in *Hugh Selwyn Mauberley* – "There died a myriad / And of the best, among them, / For an old bitch gone in the teeth, / For a botched civilization"[48] – Fitzgerald portrayed the war as shattering values and making cynicism fashionable. A famous scene in *Tender Is the Night* finds Dick Diver's coterie touring the remnants of the Somme trenches outside Beaumont Hamel in France. Noting "that this land here cost twenty lives a foot that summer" – more than one million German, French, and British died on the site between July and November 1916 – Dick lectures them on the battle's epochal significance: "This western-front business couldn't be done again, not for a long time. The young men think they could do it but they couldn't . . . This took religion and years of plenty and tremendous sureties and the exact relation between the classes . . . All my beautiful lovely safe world blew itself up here with a great gust of high explosive love" (56–7). As Dick recognizes, one victim of the war was the Romanticism that fed his belief in his special destiny. Although *Tender* does not depict combat, it is so concerned with the consequences of the Great War that it is often classified alongside Hemingway's *A Farewell to Arms* and Erich Maria Remarque's (1898–1970) *All Quiet on the Western Front* (both 1929) as a war novel.

In lamenting modern chaos, modernists sought to rationalize civilization's seeming decline by adopting theories of historical transformation that, today, can seem rather farfetched. *Ulysses* and *Finnegans Wake* (1939) reveal Joyce's fascination with the Italian philosopher Giambattista Vico (1668–1744), who formulated a three-stage cyclical model of time. In *A Vision* (1925; revised 1937) William Butler Yeats (1865–1939) proposed a complex system of evolution based on lunar phases. Other writers turned to more traditional belief systems, as when in 1927 Eliot joined the Anglican Church. Still others adhered to extreme political ideologies – most notoriously, Pound, who by the late 1930s was a virulent fascist.

Fitzgerald took his philosophical solace from Oswald Spengler (1880–1936), whose *Decline of the West* (1919–22) posited a cyclical view of civilization modeled on the four seasons. Although Fitzgerald claimed to discover Spengler while writing *The Great Gatsby*, his familiarity would have been at best secondhand, for an English translation of *Decline* was not available until 1926. A decade later, the German philosopher did inspire plans for a medieval novel entitled *The Castle* or *Philippe, Count of Darkness*, which would have catalogued the heroic traits Fitzgerald believed necessary to redeem modernity from fascism. He completed only four chapters of the allegory, three of which appeared as short stories in *Redbook* in 1934–5: "In the Darkest Hour," "The Kingdom in the Dark," and "The Count of Darkness." ("Gods of Darkness" appeared posthumously in 1941.) Dismissed as artistic debacles, these stories are nevertheless interesting, especially given that by the mid-1930s Spengler was considered a Nazi apologist – a reading that Fitzgerald vociferously rejected (*A Life in Letters* 289–90). (Although Spengler supported Hitler in 1932, he later criticized National Socialism at great personal risk.) Critics have argued that *Decline* also influenced *The Last Tycoon*, with Monroe Stahr a Philippe-style transitional hero whose battles against the forces of capitalism would herald a new artistic age in Hollywood. Although no direct textual evidence supports this interpretation, *Tycoon* does explicitly mention Spengler when Stahr's lover, Kathleen Moore, describes how a former Svengali introduced her to *Decline*: "He wanted me to read Spengler – everything was for that. All the history and philosophy and harmony was all so I could read Spengler and then I left him before we got to Spengler. At the end I think that was the chief reason he didn't want me to go" (91).

Fitzgerald was also adept at several modernist techniques. Two years before Joyce popularized the stream of consciousness style in *Ulysses*'s Molly Bloom soliloquy, he attempted a similar if more abbreviated depiction of cognitive flux in *This Side of Paradise*: "One Hundred and Twenty-seventh Street – or One Hundred and Thirty-Seventh Street . . . Seat damp . . . are clothes absorbing wetness from seat, or seat absorbing dryness from clothes? . . . Sitting on wet substance gave appendicitis, so Froggy Parker's mother said" (239). *The Great Gatsby* likewise employs the poetic dissociation of *The Waste Land*, most notably in Fitzgerald's description of the valley of ashes separating Long Island and New York City: "The gray land and the spasms of bleak dust that drift endlessly over it" (27) convey the same arid infertility as Eliot's desolate landscape of "stony rubbish . . . where the sun beats, / And the dead tree gives no shelter, the cricket no relief, / And the dry stone no sound of water."[49] The "brooding" billboard eyes of Dr T. J. Eckleburg have also drawn comparisons to *The Waste Land*'s blind prophet Tiresias, whom Eliot conjured from ancient Thebes to witness the spiritual vacuity of modern love. *Gatsby* further borrows Eliot's motif of the "unreal city" with several hallucinatory glimpses of metropolitan alienation. There is even a direct echo of Eliot's "violent hour" of the London dusk "when the human engine / waits / Like a taxi throbbing waiting" (43) in a scene that Berman calls "a set piece of modernism" in which Nick "walks through the darkened streets of the city . . . experiencing his apartness" (88): "Again at eight o'clock, when the dark lanes of the Forties were five deep and the throbbing taxi cabs bound for the theater district, I felt a sinking in my heart. Forms leaned together in taxis as they waited, and voices sang, and there was laughter from unheard jokes, and lighted cigarettes outlined unintelligible gestures inside" (46–7).

Compared with his Romantic and modernist affinities, Fitzgerald's realist influences have received comparatively little attention. His fixation with class owes a debt to Henry James, Edith Wharton (1862–1937), and other late nineteenth-century writers concerned with how privilege and money shape moral character. "The Rich Boy" is perhaps the best single example, with Anson Hunter's emotional aloofness recalling the incapacity for empathy that several Jamesian heroes suffer, from sympathetic protagonists like John Marcher in "The Beast in the Jungle" (1904) to outright villains like Gilbert Osmond in *The Portrait of a Lady* (1881). Like James, Fitzgerald was also attentive to customs. One of his most irresistible short stories, "Bernice Bobs Her Hair" (1920), is a comedy of manners that, recalling James's *Daisy Miller* (1878), roots its action in gestures of propriety that expose class affectations. In "Bernice" cutthroat competition for teen popularity reveals upper-class hypocrisy. Marjorie Harvey taunts her cousin, Bernice, into bobbing her hair, knowing that the "abomination" this flapper style represents will prevent Bernice from attending a dance, thus ending her flirtation with Marjorie's boyfriend, Warren McIntyre. In revenge, Bernice shears off Marjorie's braids while she sleeps. As in most comedies of manners, the humor arises from the disparity between the innocent peccadilloes that Bernice commits and the moral outrage they excite. Like James, Fitzgerald insists that an obsessive concern with politesse masks class prejudice and deceit.

Another realist influence involves what James called his "international theme" – the cultural differences between Europe and America that expatriation reveals. Although Fitzgerald's most famous expatriate efforts (*Tender Is the Night*, "Babylon Revisited") are modernistic, several lesser-known works focus on social interaction rather than the landscape of the mind, addressing what J. Gerald Kennedy "the nationalist ethos of Americans in Europe, their class-conscious relations with other displaced Americans, their contact as *foreigners* with 'foreign' people and languages, and their adaptation (or lack thereof) to different cultures" (*Cambridge Companion* 140). The most Jamesian of these stories is "The Hotel Child" (1930), whose plot of an American innocent imperiled by a conniving cosmopolitan inspires frequent comparisons to *Daisy Miller*. Like James's naïve flirt, Fifi Schwartz is oblivious to the affront that her liberated behavior poses to guests at the isolated Swiss hotel where her family resides. Among those offended are the "very Europeanized Americans" who consider Fifi "as much of a gratuitous outrage as a new stripe in the flag," as well as such spurious European "nobility" as Count Stanislas Borowski, who will overcome his disdain for American women only when he finds one rich enough to marry (*Short Stories* 600). When Fifi overhears the Count's anti-Semitic gibe, she realizes that Europe is not free of the bigotry that has led the Schwartzes to move from America – an important point at a time when anti-Semitism would shortly become state policy in Nazi Germany.

Fitzgerald's stylistic debt to realism generally surfaces whenever he depicts the Jazz Age's material excesses. A common realist technique is to inventory protagonists' possessions to demonstrate how taste is symbolic of character. Such passages exaggerate the specificity of detail to satirize bourgeois pretensions, as when Gustave Flaubert (1821–1880) in *Madame Bovary* (1857) catalogues the adornments that drive his heroine into ruinous debt. Similarly, Fitzgerald emphasizes Gatsby's *nouveau riche* status by itemizing the gauche decor of his mansion (a "factual imitation of some Hotel de Ville in Normandy" [8]), which includes "Marie Antoinette music-rooms and Restoration salons . . . period bedrooms swathed in rose and lavender silk and vivid with new flowers" (91), and even a library modeled on Merton College, replete "with carved English oak, and probably transported complete from some ruin overseas" (45). His arriviste "vulgarity" is apparent as well in both his clothes (he owns piles of tailored English shirts and in one scene sports "a gorgeous pink rag of a suit") and his possessions (his yellow coupé and hydroplane). His meretricious style is echoed by Tom Buchanan's mistress, Myrtle Wilson, whose fondness for faux French tapestried furniture, chiffon couture, and even the pedicures she boasts of enjoying in her and Tom's love nest reveal her essential inelegance. (As Myrtle marvels, the pedicurist, Mrs Eberhardt, "'goes around looking at people's feet in their own homes'" [28].) The enumeration of such "extravagances" reveals the realist discomfort with the emerging consumer mentality that redefined identity as a matter of having rather than being.

Some critics argue that the most valuable technique Fitzgerald learned from realism is *The Great Gatsby*'s limited point of view, which creates much of the novel's mystery. While his first two novels feature omniscient narrators who editorialize on the plot, *Gatsby* is told by a main character, Nick Carraway, who is implicated in it. Realists objected to intrusive storytelling because commentary distances readers from the action; with an observer-participant, by contrast, the audience must grapple with unstated implications. The device further heightens what realists believed was a major criterion for literature – ambiguity – by demanding that readers question the narrator's reliability. Such is the case when Nick concludes Chapter III by noting, "Every one suspects himself of at least one of the cardinal virtues, and this is mine: I am one of the few honest people that I have ever known" (59). The statement can be read two ways: either Nick is boasting of his ethical purity, making us question whether he bears more responsibility for Gatsby's tragedy than he can admit (he facilitates Gatsby's and Daisy's affair, after all), or he is ironically acknowledging his failings and implicating himself in his critique of 1920s morality. How one interprets Nick is largely determined by whether we grant him the authority to judge Gatsby, Daisy, and Tom, or whether we find him guilty of the faults he condemns in others.

Fitzgerald discovered his fourth literary mode, naturalism, through the work of brothers Frank (1870–1902) and Charles Norris (1881–1945), whose respective novels *McTeague* (1899) and *Salt* (1919) advanced a theory of environmental determinism in which hostile forces, not individual will, shape one's character. It is difficult to imagine a type of writing more distinct from Romanticism than this 1890s style, which explains why Fitzgerald's forays into it were rarely successful. His most accomplished attempt is "May Day," which depicts its characters as victims of animalistic impulses: Gordon Sterrett has taken a working-class lover, Jewel Hudson, who is blackmailing him; drunken Yale classmates Philip Dean and Peter Himmel make public spectacles of themselves; demobilized veterans Carrol Key and Gus Rose join an antisocialist riot to vent their thuggery. Only Edith Bradin possesses the "adolescent idealism" and "desire to ponder" of Fitzgerald's typical Romantic hero (*Short Stories* 110). By the story's end, Carrol has died falling thirty flights from a window, Edith's brother, Henry, the editor of a socialist newspaper, has been beaten, and Gordon has killed himself after marrying Jewel in a drunken stupor.

What makes "May Day" effective is the consistency of its characterization. Except for Edith and Henry, the narration refrains from empathizing with its principal figures. Unfortunately, this is not true of Fitzgerald's other major attempt at naturalism, *The Beautiful and Damned*. Conceived as a study in character deterioration – a concept adopted from another leading naturalist, H. L. Mencken – the book begins as an exposé of leisure-class nihilism, its putative credo voiced by Gloria Patch: "'There's only one lesson to be learned from life . . . That there's no lesson to be learned from life'" (255). Initially, Gloria is depicted as an unsympathetic figure, often through the naturalistic tactic of drawing ironic analogies to classical figures, as when Anthony imagines her on a day-long shopping spree: "Noon would come – she would hurry along Fifth Avenue, a Nordic Ganymede . . . In a thousand guises Thais would hail a cab and turn up her face for loving" (107). As Robert Sklar notes, such allusions *should* make Gloria "an interesting satire on the postwar debutante, were it not that Fitzgerald [goes] to great pains, not to satirize her, but to elevate her significance."[50] This elevation occurs through the decidedly non-ironic references to Keats's "La Belle Dame Sans Merci," which mystify the flapper as a femme fatale, a figure of erotic danger rather than parodic derision.

Anthony's characterization is equally inconsistent. Despite Fitzgerald's insistence that he revels in his "magnificent attitude of not giving a damn" (226), numerous passages detail his remorse over his indolence and alcoholism:

> Anthony Patch had ceased to be an individual of mental adventure, of curiosity, and had become an individual of bias and prejudice, with a longing to be emotionally undisturbed . . . This gradual change had taken place through the past several years, accelerated by a succession of anxieties preying on his mind. There was, first of all, the sense of waste, always dormant in his heart, now awakened by the circumstances of his position. In his moments of insecurity he was haunted by the suggestion that life might be, after all, significant.   (284)

As Bruccoli suggests, such passages find Fitzgerald "credit[ing] Anthony and Gloria with a certain integrity of irresponsibility, casting them as victims of philistia" (*Epic Grandeur* 179). The inconsistency may not only arise from what such passages say but in the psychological depth they confer on the Patches. In most naturalistic works characters lack insight into their predicament; whether victims of their surroundings or instruments of it, they remain obtuse and unreflective. Yet Anthony and Gloria both "brood [over] wasted opportunities" so often that Fitzgerald is never able to sustain the irony that is naturalism's chief tool for dramatizing the beastliness of existence (371).

Another problem with *The Beautiful and Damned*'s naturalism is the imprecise etiology of the Patches' decline. Most naturalistic works dramatize environmental determination through a single de-evolutionary force, whether bourgeois professionalism in *McTeague* or industrialism in *Vandover, the Brute* (1914), another influential Frank Norris novel. In more political examples the protagonist's defeat comes at the hands of a commercial monopoly that symbolizes capitalist inequities, *à la* the meatpacking industry in Upton Sinclair's *The Jungle* (1906). Yet *Beautiful* attributes the Patches' deterioration to a variety of mainsprings: inherited money, marriage, the prodigality encouraged by modern consumerism, indolence, and alcoholism. Curiously, the cause that prompts the loudest protest is the aging process. Fitzgerald repeatedly interrupts the plot to lament the loss of vitality that comes with growing older: "By the late twenties . . . we cease to be impulsive, convincible men, interested in what is ethically true by fine margins, we substitute rules of conduct for ideas of integrity, we value safety above romance, we become quite unconsciously pragmatic" (284). This age consciousness becomes unintentionally comic at the climactic moment when Gloria must gauge the severity of her husband's decline: "He was thirty-three – he looked forty" (444). An argument could be made that senescence *is* the kind of deterministic force that naturalists believed was the downfall of humanity; when compared with the lust, greed, and exploitative violence in the Norrises and Sinclair, however, it is simply too amorphous to make for a compelling villain. Most critics dismiss it as an expression of Fitzgerald's own anxieties about lost youth rather than a grave tragedy.

Style and point of view

Along with Hemingway and William Faulkner (1897–1962), Fitzgerald is considered one of the three most distinctive American prose stylists of the twentieth century. But whereas his peers are known respectively for their stoic sparsity and psychological elaboration, his expressive habits are harder to pigeonhole. His lyricism is his most recognizable characteristic, yet critics by no means agree about its purpose or effect. While many rank the ending of *The Great Gatsby* as one of the most moving passages in American literature, they also insist that Fitzgerald's emotional intensity often swamped his subject matter. Milton R. Stern argues that between *This Side of Paradise* and *The Last Tycoon* his style "progress[ed]" from "lyrical celebration" and "associational evocation" to more "concretely actualized scene[s]" – or, more bluntly, from "luxurious literary showing off" to "beautiful efficiency."[51] Whether this development constitutes "progress" is a matter of opinion, yet Stern is correct to note that Fitzgerald's lyrical gifts and his dramatic skills could work at cross purposes. The friction is apparent in descriptive passages as well as in his preference for an omniscient point of view, which allowed him to comment on his unfolding plots.

In Fitzgerald's early love stories, lyrical evocations are notable for their sumptuous overstatement, as in the opening of "The Ice Palace": "The sunlight dripped over the house like golden paint over an art jar, and the freckling shadows here and there only intensified the rigor of the bath of light" (*Short Stories*

48). The unconventional simile and verbs introduce the theme of Southern languor embodied by heroine Sally Carrol Happer, who by the story's end has returned to the "quite enervating yet oddly comforting heat" of Tarleton, Georgia, after a gelid journey to suitor Harry Bellamy's Minnesota hometown. Similarly, "The Offshore Pirate" suggests how Fitzgerald's palette creates an almost Day-Glo luminosity that renders the setting every bit as fantastic as the faux-kidnapping plot:

> This unlikely story begins on a sea that was a blue dream, as colorful as blue silk-stockings, and beneath a sky as blue as irises of children's eyes. From the western half of the sky the sun was shying little golden disks at the sea – if you gazed intently enough you could see them skip from wave tip to wave tip until they joined a broad collar of golden coin that was collecting half a mile out and would eventually be a dazzling sunset. (*Short Stories* 70)

This vividness is not always so larkish; in tragedies like *Tender Is the Night*, it creates a hallucinatory atmosphere, as when Dick and Rosemary first kiss in a Parisian taxi:

> As lovers now they fell ravenously on the quick seconds while outside the taxi windows the green and cream twilight faded, and the fire-red, gas-blue, ghost-green signs began to shine smokily through the tranquil rain. It was nearly six, the streets were in movement, the bistros gleamed, and the Place de la Concorde moved by in pink majesty as the cab turned north. (74)

Such lyricism is rarely controversial when describing a setting. It bothers critics, however, when it characterizes habits of mind, as when Dick realizes that his need for admiration has caused his downfall:

> His love for Nicole and Rosemary, his friendship with Abe North, with Tommy Barban in the broken universe of the war's ending – in such contacts the personalities had seemed to press up so close to him that he became the personality itself – there seemed some necessity of taking all or nothing; it was as if for the remainder of his life he was condemned to carry with him the egos of certain people, early met and early loved, and to be only as complete as they were complete themselves. There was some element of loneliness involved – so easy to be loved – so hard to love. (245)

According to Philip Rahv, such passages "console and caress" characters with "soft words uttered in [a] furry voice" that "varnishes rather than reveals the essential facts" (*Critical Reception* 316–17). In other words, the rhetorical intricacy is presumed to cloud rather than clarify Fitzgerald's point. Yet it is worth asking whether an "unvarnished" style would suit *Tender Is the Night*. Psychological insight in the novel is convoluted, self-deceptive, and contradictory because Fitzgerald is depicting the modern self as fragmented and uncertain. To portray characters' thoughts in a straightforward fashion would have contradicted the book's premise.

Because Fitzgerald's lyricism is usually conspicuous, it is easy to overlook his strengths as a scenarist. Few critics, for example, commend his dialogue, whose wit arguably accounts for much of his early appeal. Ardita Farnam's first exchange with her buccaneer-suitor in "The Offshore Pirate" displays his talent for repartee:

> "Narcissus ahoy!" he called politely.
> "What's the idea of all the discord?" demanded Ardita cheerfully. "Is this the varsity crew from the county nut farm?" . . .
> "The women and children will be spared!" he said briskly. "All crying babies will be immediately drowned and all males put in double irons!"
> Digging her hands excitedly down into the pockets of her dress Ardita stared at him, speechless with astonishment . . .
> "Well, I'll be a son of a gun!" she said dazedly.
> They eyed each other coolly.
> "Do you surrender the ship?"
> "Is this an outburst of wit?" demanded Ardita. "Are you an idiot – or just being initiated into some fraternity?"
> "I asked if you surrendered the ship."
> "I thought the country was dry," said Ardita disdainfully. "Have you been drinking finger-nail enamel? You better get off this yacht!"
>
> (*Short Stories* 75)

Suffice it to say that before Fitzgerald, few *Saturday Evening Post* stories referenced "idiots" or "drowned babies." By pruning the formality of Victorian dialogue and allowing his lovers to speak in adolescent slang, Fitzgerald turned conversation into a vehicle for snappy patter and verbal parrying, two essential components of his jazziness.

Another misunderstood aspect of Fitzgerald's style is his preferred point of view for narrating his fiction. Whether writing in the first or the third person, he typically assumed an omniscient perspective that allowed him to "get the verisimilitude of a first person narrative with a Godlike knowledge of all that happens to my characters" (*A Life in Letters* 410). The opening of "The Curious Case of Benjamin Button" suggests the chatty extremes to which he could tend:

> As long ago as 1860 it was the proper thing to be born at home. At present, so I am told, the high gods of medicine have decreed that the first cries of the young shall be uttered upon the anesthetic air of a hospital, preferably a fashionable one. So young Mr. and Mrs. Roger Button were fifty years ahead of style when they decided, one day in the summer of 1860, that their first baby should be born in a hospital. Whether this anachronism had any bearing upon the astonishing history I am about to set down will never be known.
>
> I shall tell you what occurred, and let you judge for yourself.
>
> (*Short Stories* 159)

Because modernist aesthetics discouraged such loquaciousness, critics consider this habit a foible. Only in *The Great Gatsby*, "Babylon Revisited," and a smattering of other stories, they insist, was Fitzgerald able to resist the temptation to editorialize and instead intensify the drama by focusing it through an observer-narrator like Nick Carraway or a third-person character like Charlie Wales. Yet his "intrusiveness" actually serves valuable ends. First, a prominent narrator focuses audience attention by explicitly articulating the point, as when "The Rich Boy" insists that Anson Hunter's story is not meant to excite class envy: "There is a rich boy, and this is his and not his brothers' story . . . If I wrote about his brother I should have to begin by attacking all the lies the poor have told about the rich and the rich have told about themselves" (*Short Stories* 318). Elsewhere, commentary serves a philosophic purpose by abstracting general human truths from the storyline. While describing Anthony's and Gloria's courtship in *The Beautiful and Damned*, Fitzgerald pauses to consider the difficulties of controlling one's image:

> The growth of intimacy is like that. First one gives off his best picture, the bright and finished product mended with bluff and falsehood and humor. Then more details are required and one paints a second portrait, and a third – before long the best lines cancel out – and the secret is exposed at last; the plane of the pictures have intermingled and given us away, and though we paint and paint we can no longer sell a picture. We must be satisfied with hoping that such fatuous accounts of ourselves as we make to our wives and children and business associates are accepted as true.   (111)

Such ruminations seem extraneous because their purpose is not dramatic. They aim, rather, to establish a relationship with the reader – an ambition, again, that was central to Fitzgerald's early appeal. "Intrusions" were the chief means by which he negotiated his role as a generational spokesman. They enabled him to address peers and parents simultaneously, justifying flapper mores while ribbing offended elders. In "Bernice Bobs Her Hair" the narrator pauses to explain why debutantes enjoy being "frequently cut in on" at dances: "Youth in this jazz-nourished generation is temperamentally restless, and the idea of foxtrotting more than one full foxtrot with the same girl is distasteful, not to say odious. When it comes to several dances and the intermissions between she can be quite sure that a young man, once relieved, will never tread on her wayward toes again" (*Short Stories* 28). As late as the Basil and Josephine stories, which postdate the flapper fad by a good half-decade, Fitzgerald continued this habit, as if protecting adolescent characters from adult misconceptions. Thus when Josephine Perry flirts with Anthony Harker in "First Blood," he defends her impulsiveness: "She did not plan; she merely let herself go, and the overwhelming life in her did the rest. It is only when youth is gone and experience has given us a cheap sort of courage that most of us realize how simple things are" (*Basil and Josephine* 235).

One reason why the purpose of such commentary is not always clear is that their interpolation into the narrative is not always seamless. Sometimes they read like clumsy stage directions, as if Fitzgerald were using them to keep characters and plots straight in his own mind. Critics often point to a perspectival transition in *Tender Is the Night* as an example of how clunky omniscience can be: "To resume Rosemary's point of view . . ." (28). *The Last Tycoon* includes several similarly awkward moments that reflect Fitzgerald's uncertainty over narrator Cecelia Brady's role in the drama. After a romantic interlude between Stahr and Kathleen Moore in Episode 13, the next scene begins, "This is Cecelia taking up the narrative in person" (77), while Episode 15 begins, "This is Cecelia taking up the story" (99). It is unclear whether Fitzgerald would have excised such jarring moments had he lived to complete the book; while most critics believe he would, it certainly would not have been out of character to leave them. In the end, narrative style was a way to convey personality, which is why he is not only a vocal but an ingratiating presence in his work.

Chapter 4

Critical reception

A survey of Fitzgerald criticism demonstrates how aesthetic values vary from age to age. The reasons why some reviewers celebrated *The Great Gatsby* in 1925 as an improvement on his previous novels are not the same ones that led the succeeding generation to pronounce it a classic. Nor do the criteria by which Fitzgerald was reclaimed from obscurity in the 1940s bear much relation to those currently employed to gauge his canonicity. In his lifetime the main question surrounding him concerned his "sensibility" – specifically, his maturity. In the immediate decades after his death, sensibility as a literary quality was considered too subjective, so critics focused on the work instead of the author's personality. These "formalist" readings (so called because they are concerned with the text's form or design) remained popular for another twenty years, after which they were criticized for ignoring the historical context. Today most Fitzgerald scholars read his work against the backdrop of the 1920s and 1930s, arguing that they have much to teach us about those eras.

Contemporary reviewers: admirers, detractors, and the problem of maturity

Fitzgerald entered the public spotlight as much as a pundit as a *littérateur*. Although his *métier* was fiction, many reviewers were more interested in what he had to say about his generation's sociology. Headlines of *This Side of Paradise* (1920) reviews tell the story: "A Chronicle of Youth By Youth" read *The Bookman*, while the *Philadelphia Evening Public Ledger* announced "Youth Writes About Youth" and the *Boston Herald* opted for an even more basic description: "About Flappers." Perhaps the cleverest came from the *St. Louis Post-Dispatch*, which cried, "Good Afternoon! Have You a Little P. D. in Your Home?" – a "P. D." being *Paradise* slang for a "Popular Daughter" or flapper. Although a handful of reviewers heralded the emergence of a new talent ("Whew!" the *Chicago Daily News* exclaimed. "That Boy Can Write!"), most focused on the novel's saucier details, including the shocking revelation that teenagers like to drink alcohol and to pet.[1] Because of his association with such frippery, Fitzgerald was stereotyped as a "facile" talent. Even after he realized his artistic potential in *The Great Gatsby* (1925), some critics assumed that the revelries it depicts (drinking and adultery) meant that he had yet to mature. As late as *Tender Is the Night* (1934), published when Fitzgerald was thirty-seven, debate continued over whether he had graduated to "adult" concerns or whether he was, as the *New York Herald Tribune*'s Lewis Gannett put it, "still writing of women beautiful and damned, and sad young men, and of a jazz age far this side of paradise" (*Critical Reception* 296).

One critic who could have raised Fitzgerald's stock did much to deflate it. Fitzgerald first met Edmund Wilson at Princeton, where they worked together on the student magazine, the *Nassau Literary Review*, and collaborated on an undergraduate club musical, *The Third Eye*, in 1915. Fitzgerald admired Wilson's formidable erudition and in late 1919 sought his opinion of *This Side of Paradise*. Wilson did not review the novel, but in private correspondence he doubted whether Fitzgerald was an intellectual, congratulating him instead for writing a "burlesque" that would make him "a very popular trashy novelist."[2] The judgment would not vary during Fitzgerald's lifetime; Wilson's comments are usually a "mixture of friendly derision, backhanded compliments and faint praise" in which he commends Fitzgerald's satirical wit while criticizing him as unlettered and undisciplined.[3] His 1922 *Bookman* review of *The Beautiful and Damned* evinces his condescension: "It has been said . . . that to meet F. Scott Fitzgerald is to think of a stupid old woman with whom someone has left a diamond . . . Everyone is surprised that such an ignorant old woman should possess so valuable a jewel." Wilson then enumerated his flaws: "He has been given imagination without intellectual control of it; he has been given the desire for beauty without an aesthetic ideal; and he has been given a gift for expression without very many ideas to express."[4] As such, Fitzgerald was best suited for "lighthearted high spirits," a point Wilson reiterated that same year in a *Vanity Fair* review of *Tales of the Jazz Age* (1922) when he commended his "mastery of the nuances of the ridiculous" and his plots' "spontaneous nonsense." Most viciously, Wilson insisted that Fitzgerald was unintentionally funny when he aspired to tragedy: "What was my surprise when I finished [the story 'The Lees of Happiness'] to discover it was intended to be serious. Yes,

Fitzgerald is our most incalculable of novelists . . . Just when you think the joke is going to be on you, it may turn out to be on him" (*Critical Reception* 152). So skewed was Wilson's view that he made the preposterous claim that *The Vegetable*, Fitzgerald's disastrous attempt at theater, was "one of the best things he has done" – an opinion that, whether now or in 1923, one would have been hard pressed to have seconded (*Critical Reception* 182).

Tellingly, Wilson did not review *The Great Gatsby*, reserving his praise for private correspondence.[5] His last major assessment of Fitzgerald before 1941 was a *New Republic* parody entitled "The Delegate from Great Neck," published in 1924 as Fitzgerald was composing his third novel. The article mocks Fitzgerald's reputation as an *enfant terrible* by imagining a conversation with the genteel literary critic Van Wyck Brooks (1886–1963), to whom Fitzgerald boasts of his lust for publicity, his ignorance of Henry James, and of his need to write "rotten stuff that bores me and makes me depressed" so that he can afford to live in New York's chicest suburb (*In His Own Time* 428). Throughout the late 1920s and 1930s, Wilson built a reputation as the "dean of American critics" thanks to several studies that helped to define the modernist tradition. Significantly, Fitzgerald is mentioned only in passing, if at all, in *Axel's Castle* (1931), *The Triple Thinkers* (1938), and *The Wound and the Bow* (1941); Wilson simply did not put his colleague in the same category as James Joyce, Gertrude Stein, or even Ernest Hemingway.[6] Only after Fitzgerald died would he reassess his opinion. Oddly enough, he would become a leading force in the Fitzgerald revival of the 1940s and 1950s, thanks to his editing of *The Last Tycoon* (1941) and *The Crack-Up* (1945). "I patronized Scott," Wilson admitted in 1944, "and said a lot of things about him [early on] that *The Great Gatsby* was to prove false" (qtd. in *Edmund Wilson* 226). In the end, the reasons for his long-held ambivalence were as personal as literary. As one biographer notes, "The reserved Wilson was put off by Fitzgerald's [drunken] antics" and resented his fame.[7]

Another contemporary who underestimated Fitzgerald was H. L. Mencken, the newspaper columnist and *The Smart Set* co-editor known for his caustic criticism of the American middle class, which he famously dubbed the "Booboisie." Mencken was a little more generous in his estimation than Wilson: instead of a lightweight satirist, Mencken felt that Fitzgerald had the makings of an imposing social critic who (not unlike Mencken himself) could expose the hypocrisies of American life – but only if he disassociated himself from the *Saturday Evening Post*. Mencken's review of *Flappers and Philosophers* (1920) was one of the first to note how Fitzgerald's pursuit of both critical and commercial success resulted in a split personality: "Fitzgerald is curiously ambidextrous. Will he proceed via the first part of *This Side of Paradise* to the cold groves of beautiful letters, or will he proceed via 'Head and Shoulders' into the sunshine that warms [popular authors such as] Robert W. Chambers and Harold McGrath?" Mencken's disdain for love stories led him to dismiss "The Offshore Pirate" and other flapper tales as "confections" while hailing pieces with the potential to spark controversy. One such story was the now-forgotten "Benediction" (1920), which he singled out for "[bringing] down the maledictions of the Jesuits" and nearly getting *The Smart Set,* in which it originally appeared, "barred from the Knights of Columbus-camp libraries" (*Critical Reception* 48). Mencken's preference for agonistic writing also led him to hail *The Beautiful and Damned* as Fitzgerald's best work, for its critique of the idle rich would "give a shock to all the fluffier and more flapperish Fitzgeraldistas" (*Critical Reception* 106). Significantly, his tastes prevented him from appreciating the nuances of more complex efforts, especially *The Great Gatsby,* which he labeled "a glorified anecdote," an "obviously unimportant" story most interesting for its prose style than for its historical significance (*Critical Reception* 211–12). Not unlike Wilson, Mencken was prejudiced against Fitzgerald from exposure to his carousing; his posthumously published autobiography, *My Life as Author and Editor* (1993), contains many anecdotes that explain his low estimation. Although *My Life* revises his opinion of *Gatsby,* Mencken reveals little fondness for Fitzgerald's other work, even condemning *Tender Is the Night* as "poor stuff indeed" – a judgment he might have a hard time justifying since, as he admits, he "did not even read it."[8]

Despite Wilson's and Mencken's dismissive views, advocates, including two St Paul acquaintances, the married couple Thomas and Woodward (Peggy) Boyd (1898–1935 and 1898–1965 respectively), countered Fitzgerald's image as a mere "flapper novelist." Boyd's 1922 newspaper interview "Literary Libels" offers an interesting rejoinder to Wilson's *Bookman* review: not only does Fitzgerald proffer opinions on a range of authors and books (thereby refuting claims that he was intellectually shallow), but Boyd describes his writing process, even noting his elaborate revisions and his use of a thesaurus to prove his professionalism (*In His Own Time* 245–54). Meanwhile, his wife's assessment of *Tales of the Jazz Age,* "The Fitzgerald Legend," praises the sentimentality of "The Lees of Happiness" (1920), the very story Wilson ridiculed: "I read it . . . and wept over it. This is very unlike anything else he has ever done." Instead of denouncing his plots as "nonsense," she insists that the carefully constructed twists of "The Camel's Back" and "The Jelly-Bean" (both 1920) show "a definite mastery of his tools" (*Critical Reception* 160). The Boyds' spirited defenses did little to influence critical perceptions, however, partly because they wrote for a regional newspaper (the *St Paul Daily News*), and partly because their extolments were considered payback for Fitzgerald's having helped each to publish a novel with Scribner's – her *The Love Legend* in 1922 and his *Through the Wheat* in 1923.

Not until *The Great Gatsby* could supporters make a persuasive case for Fitzgerald the artist. Gilbert Seldes (1893–1970), author of the important popular culture study *The Seven Lively Arts* (1924), found his growth so impressive that he reviewed the novel twice. In *The Dial* he noted two improvements over previous Fitzgerald efforts: "The novel is composed as an artistic structure, and it exposes, again for the first time, an interesting temperament." Significantly, that temperament is the antithesis of what Wilson cited as the author's strength: "Fitzgerald has ceased to content himself with a satiric report on the outside of American life and with considerable irony has attacked the spirit underneath" (*Critical Reception* 240). A few months later in *New Criterion*, Seldes lauded *Gatsby* as a "brilliant work," insisting that Fitzgerald "has certainly the best chance, at this moment, of becoming our finest artist in fiction" (*Critical Reception* 243). Similarly, William Rose Benét (1886–1950) declared in the *Saturday Review of Literature* that Fitzgerald had tapped the "depth of philosophy," demonstrating a "thoroughly matured craftsmanship" (*Critical Reception* 220). Yet, despite the broad recognition that, as the *New York World*'s Laurence Stallings (1894–1968) put it, *Gatsby* revealed an "interest in the color and sweep of prose, in the design and integrity of the novel, in the development of character, like nothing else he has attempted" (*Critical Reception* 203), just as many critics *failed* to appreciate his growth. "F. Scott Fitzgerald's Latest a Dud" (*Critical Reception* 195) read the headline of another *New York World* review, while Ruth Hale of the *Brooklyn Daily Eagle* promised to "bind myself to read one Scott Fitzgerald book a week for the rest of my life" if a reader could "find me one trace of magic, life, irony, romance or mysticism in all of *The Great Gatsby*" (*Critical Reception* 197). These critics proved blind to the novel's symbolic import; they either attacked the characters' morality, denouncing Gatsby and Daisy as "sordid," "cheap," and "tawdry," or, like Mencken, they found the plot negligible.

Perhaps the most compelling lesson of *The Great Gatsby* reviews is the difficulty of altering one's public image. Nearly every review, pro or con, compares the novel to *This Side of Paradise*, as do many commentaries on the three remaining books that Fitzgerald published in his lifetime. "The precosity [*sic*] that glittered in the work of young Mr. Fitzgerald when he used to write exclusively about petting and orange juice, has acquired a deepening strain of understanding," *Time* said of *All the Sad Young Men* (1926). Yet "however thoughtful these days," it decided, Fitzgerald "has sprouted no lugubrious grey chin-wisps" (*Critical Reception* 165). Such comments did little to revise opinions. Edward Weeks in the *Atlantic Monthly* did not find much difference between *Paradise* and *Tender Is the Night*, the two Fitzgerald novels that on the surface have the least in common: "Mr. Fitzgerald is a romantic crying in the wilderness of sophistication. He was a romantic in 1920 and he is one today" (*Critical Reception* 287). Among *Tender* reviewers, only Seldes was unequivocally positive, proclaiming it "the great novel" of Fitzgerald's career: "He has gone behind generations, old or new, and created his own image of human beings" (*Critical Reception* 293). Most reviewers found *Tender* fractured and incohesive, reinforcing the opinion that, save for *The Great Gatsby*, Fitzgerald was not adept at novelistic structure.

One such reviewer, Malcolm Cowley (1898–1989), would play a major role in the Fitzgerald revival, though before the 1940s he considered him a minor figure. Unlike such now-obscure names as William Slater Brown (1897–1997) and S. Foster Damon (1893–1971), Fitzgerald did not make Cowley's shortlist of peers predicted to define the era in his early essay "This Youngest Generation" (1921). His reviews of *All the Sad Young Men* and *Tender Is the Night* make no mention of *The Great Gatsby*, leading subsequent critics to wonder whether he had read it at the time. In 1934 Cowley published his generational memoir, *Exile's Return*, "the first book of its kind to give an authoritative design of interpretation to the social, historical, and literary forces at work on the lost generation."[9] The first edition mentions Fitzgerald exactly four times, far fewer than either Ernest Hemingway or John Dos Passos. (The 1951 revision, by contrast, cites him eleven times, still fewer than Hemingway but more than Dos Passos.) Despite this apparently low opinion, Cowley's scattered comments foreshadow important critical trends. His *Tender* review introduced the idea that Fitzgerald suffered from a "double personality" that "enabled him to portray American society from the inside, and yet at the same time surround it with an atmosphere of magic and romance that exists only in the eyes of people watching at the carriage entrance as the guests arrive in limousines" (*Critical Reception* 324–35). In the 1950s Cowley would elaborate upon this thesis, arguing that the author's "maximum of critical attachment" combined with his "maximum of immersion" to become his "distinguishing mark."[10] The "double personality" theory would subsequently be called upon to explain Fitzgerald's moral ambivalence toward his subject matter, best represented by Nick Carraway's ability in *Gatsby* to simultaneously partake in and comment upon the action. In *Tender*'s case, however, Cowley felt that "the division" was a "liability." He would attempt to redress the novel's putative failure "to give the feeling of being complete in itself" by editing a 1951 edition in which Books I and II were printed in reverse order so the story was told in chronological sequence.

The misperceptions distorting Fitzgerald's reputation are also present in his obituaries. Repeatedly, eulogists focused on the social impact of *This Side of Paradise*, whether positively ("One can reread it today and find in it far more than a dazzlingly authentic portrait of a vanished day and a forgotten youth," the *Baltimore Sun* insisted) or negatively ("Fitzgerald dealt with a group who were . . . merely petulant, because no one had invented a gin that didn't cause hangover," groused the *New York World-Telegram*). They debated whether he had fulfilled or failed his promise; questioned whether *The Great Gatsby* was a masterpiece or merely his best work ("Not a book for the ages," the *New York Times* opined, "but it caught superbly the spirit of a decade"); and agreed that with his death the Jazz Age officially became antiquated, as opposed to simply irrelevant ("That [his books] are already to a great extent unread is perhaps the best testimonial to the fact that the kind of society they portrayed is even now retreating into history," declared the *Saturday Review of Literature*) (*Critical Reception* 471, 473, 470, 476). To elevate *Gatsby* to the status of a classic, the next generation would have to shift the discussion from Fitzgerald's personality to his artistry.

The Fitzgerald revival: universalizing themes and scouring for symbols

Fitzgerald's critical rehabilitation began in 1941 with two key events: a two-part *New Republic* colloquy (March 3 and 17) featuring contributions by Cowley and several influential admirers, including John O'Hara (1905–1970) and Glenway Wescott; and the publication that October of *The Last Tycoon*, which, as Jackson R. Bryer notes, reviewers "greeted . . . with more uniformly positive responses than they had directed at any of his books during his lifetime."[11] Featuring nary a flapper or dissolute beau, *Tycoon* found its author, the *Washington Post* claimed, "shak[ing] off the incubus of that spirit of the Twenties which he himself helped so largely to create, and . . . mak[ing] that step forward for which his audience so eagerly waited." While some critics admitted to being swayed by the pathos of Fitzgerald's premature death, most agreed with Clifton Fadiman in the *New Yorker*, who insisted that "this man . . . hardly deserves to be ticketed as the laureate of the Jazz Age and then forgotten." Most presciently, Stephen Vincent Benét (1898–1943) predicted that the inclusion of *The Great Gatsby* and several of his best short stories ("May Day," 1920, "The Diamond as Big as the Ritz," 1922, "Absolution," 1924) in *Tycoon* would lead to Fitzgerald's rediscovery: "The evidence is in . . . This is not a legend, this is a reputation – and, seen in perspective, it may be one of the most secure reputations of our time" (*Critical Reception* 369, 368, 375–6).

For the reputation to outshine the legend, advocates had to universalize his themes to demonstrate that they were meaningful beyond the 1920s. Cowley thus insisted that his best works "succeeded in detaching themselves from his decade," while Dos Passos rebuked eulogists who had described Fitzgerald's popularity as a fad: "To write about the life of a man as important to American letters as the author of *The Great Gatsby* in terms of last summer's styles in ladies' hats, showed an incomprehension of what [literature] was all about . . . Fortunately there was enough of [*Tycoon*] written to still these silly yappings. The celebrity was dead. The novelist remained."[12] In the late 1940s the first academic to specialize in Fitzgerald, Arthur Mizener (1907–1988), published a quartet of articles that assessed his literary and moral qualities. By arguing that Fitzgerald's work is "a comment on humanity at large," Mizener was instrumental in making him respectable both to study and to teach.[13]

After *The Crack-Up*'s publication and then again when Mizener's *The Far Side of Paradise* (1951) – the first Fitzgerald biography – became a surprise bestseller, leading intellectuals began to specify these aspects of "humanity at large." The variety of answers demonstrated the unappreciated diversity of Fitzgerald's interests. In *The Liberal Imagination* (1950) Lionel Trilling (1905–1975) insisted that he was "a moralist to the core" and that he was "the last notable writer to affirm the Romantic fantasy . . . of life committed to, or thrown away for, some ideal of self." In *After the Lost Generation* (1951), John W. Aldridge (1925–) limned his "tragic sense" of life, noting his heroes' sensitivity to the "deeper disturbances in Paradise . . . for the beautiful there is always damnation; for every tenderness there is always the black horror of night; for all the bright young men there is sadness." Perhaps the period's most significant essay was Marius Bewley's "Scott Fitzgerald's Criticism of America" (1954), which placed the author "in a line with the greatest masters of American prose." Arguing that *The Great Gatsby*'s subject is the American Dream, Bewley insisted that the plot critiqued the "romantic enlargement of the possibilities of life on a level at which the material and spiritual have become inextricably confused."[14] If such a thesis today seems cliché, it is only because so many subsequent commentators, knowingly or not, have been so thoroughly influenced by it.

Most of these "recuperative" essays were openly subjective and deduced Fitzgerald's philosophy of life from his trademark themes. The interpretive practice known as New Criticism, by contrast, advocated close readings of texts, believing that meaning is produced through literary technique rather than authorial intent. Spearheaded by John Crowe Ransom (1888–1974),

Robert Penn Warren (1905–1989), and Cleanth Brooks (1906–1994), formalism became the 1950s' dominant method of explication for two reasons: 1) its concentration on the internal properties of art democratized literary study by allowing critics lacking access to the research materials demanded by traditional scholarship to formulate "legitimate" readings; and 2) it provided a method for teaching literature that, ostensibly, possessed the rigor and objectivity of science. The richness of Fitzgerald's prose style made him a natural for exponents of New Criticism. While a title like "Telephone Symbolism in *The Great Gatsby*" (1954) suggests that some strove a little *too* hard for significant patterns of imagery, formalists were nevertheless instrumental in making it acceptable to explore the inviting implications of Fitzgerald's style. Essays such as Tom Burnam's "The Eyes of Dr. Eckleburg: A Re-examination of *The Great Gatsby*" (1952), Douglas Taylor's "*The Great Gatsby*: Style and Myth" (1953), and Robert Ornstein's "Scott Fitzgerald's Fable of East and West" (1956) established themes that would be analyzed for years to come, including the modern world's lack of spirituality, the chivalric and even Christological nature of Gatsby's quest for Daisy, and the geographic mythologies evoked by the setting. Two 1957 essays – Thomas A. Hanzo's "The Theme and the Narrator of *The Great Gatsby*" and Jerome Thale's "The Narrator as Hero" – inaugurated a debate over the reliability of Nick Carraway's narration that continues even today.[15]

In its purest form, New Criticism eschewed biography, insisting that interpretation should evaluate the unity of art. In practice, Fitzgerald critics plied its techniques to assess such authorial concerns as literary development, influences and sources, and *The Great Gatsby*'s thematic relevance to other canonical works, whether T. S. Eliot's *The Waste Land* (1922), Charles Dickens's (1812–1870) *Great Expectations* (1861), or Mark Twain's (1835–1910) *Huckleberry Finn* (1885). The first full-length Fitzgerald study, James E. Miller's *The Fictional Technique of Scott Fitzgerald* (1957; revised as *F. Scott Fitzgerald: His Art and His Technique*, 1964), charts the author's growth from *This Side of Paradise* to *Gatsby*, exploring how he came "to see his material objectively." Sparking this growth was a shift from the discursive approach of H. G. Wells (1866–1946) to the more dramatic, presentational style of Henry James. Another influential study from this period, Richard D. Lehan's *F. Scott Fitzgerald and the Craft of Fiction* (1966), likewise assesses how fictional technique indicates Fitzgerald's "developing imagination" from 1920 to 1925. The emphasis on growth suggests why such analyses regard *Tender Is the Night* as "defective": the formalist preference for unity prevented appreciation of its inchoate qualities.[16] For *Tender* to gain its critical due, two things would have to happen. First, critics would have to broaden their focus to understand its concern with the seismic ruptures of historical change (as opposed to the social obstacles that Gatsby faces) – a point marvelously made by Milton R. Stern in *The Golden Moment* (1970).[17] Second, critics would have to recognize that the novel's fragmented structure reflected the influence of a different type of modernism, one modeled upon Joyce's *Ulysses* (1922) and Virginia Woolf's (1882–1941) *Mrs. Dalloway* (1925) instead of James and Joseph Conrad (1857–1924). In this mode the discontinuity of form evokes the chaos of the modern world. Its importance in redeeming *Tender* from its reputation as a "brilliant failure" is the subject both of Stern's *Tender Is the Night: The Broken Universe* (1994) and J. Gerald Kennedy's *Imagining Paris: Exile, Writing, and American Identity* (1993).

By the 1970s, formalism had fallen out of fashion as scholarship diversified and, in response to the tumult of the day, turned increasingly political. Fitzgerald studies has largely avoided the rancor that can result when critics assess writers' ideological inclinations; commentators rarely condemn Fitzgerald as misogynistic or racist, as often happens with Hemingway and William Faulkner, even when finding fault with his attitudes toward women and minorities. If post-1960s interpretive trends share a single impetus, it is the effort to "historicize" Fitzgerald – to read him, that is, within the very context of the 1920s from which the revivalists sought to disassociate him.

Modern Fitzgerald studies: historical turns and biographical controversies

The most influential branch of criticism since the 1960s is the oldest and, unfortunately, the least appreciated. Without textual studies, literary analysis would be impossible, for reliable interpretation requires knowledge of how a work developed from conception to publication. Too often, beginning readers assume that studying drafts and typescripts is a dreary matter of tallying typos and collating wayward commas. Yet the first manuscript study of Fitzgerald, Matthew J. Bruccoli's *The Composition of* Tender Is the Night (1963), demonstrates how essential this scholarly branch is to avoiding the half-truths and conventional assumptions that can tarnish a reputation. Assessing some 3,500 pages of manuscript, Bruccoli challenges the "lugubrious balderdash" surrounding the book, including the presumption

> that Fitzgerald worked on *Tender Is the Night* so long that he rewrote it
> to death; that he changed the plot without changing his characters and
> thereby introduced a basic confusion into the book; that after years of
> fumbling with a subject that was too profound for him, he hastily and
> carelessly assembled the book; that (and this is inevitable) he wrote
> *Tender Is the Night* drunk.[18]

Bruccoli subsequently produced composition studies of both *The Great Gatsby* (1973) and *The Last Tycoon* (1977); equally important, he oversaw the publication of the eighteen-volume *F. Scott Fitzgerald: Manuscripts* (1990–1), which extended the opportunity for textual studies to scholars and students without access to Fitzgerald's papers, which since 1950 have been housed at Princeton. As Bruccoli notes, the manuscripts "dispel the myth of Fitzgerald's irresponsibility. They demonstrate he was a painstaking reviser, a process he extended into the proof stage."[19]

At the time of his *Tender Is the Night* study, Bruccoli (1931–) was the founder of the *Fitzgerald Newsletter* (1958–68), the first publication devoted to building a community of Fitzgerald scholars. (It was followed in 1969 by the *Hemingway/Fitzgerald Annual*, which also ran for a decade.) Bruccoli soon succeeded Mizener as the leading authority in the field, thanks to his indefatigable editing of some three dozen volumes, including previously uncollected stories (*Bits of Paradise* [1973] and *The Price Was High* [1979]), correspondence (*As Ever, Scott Fitz* – [1972], *A Life in Letters* [1994]), and personal ephemera (*Ledger* [1973], *Notebooks* [1978]). If only for making these primary resources available, Bruccoli deserves the appreciation of every Fitzgerald aficionado. Yet he has also authored the standard biography, *Some Sort of Epic Grandeur* (1981; revised 1991 and 2002). While some consider Mizener's *The Far Side of Paradise* a more entertaining read, *Epic Grandeur* remains the most reliable resource for a simple reason: it keeps to the facts, avoiding the prurient speculation that has come to dominate biographical studies. Flawed examples of the genre such as James R. Mellow's *Invented Lives: Scott and Zelda Fitzgerald* (1984) and Kendall Taylor's *Sometimes Madness is Wisdom: Scott and Zelda Fitzgerald: A Marriage* (2001) demonstrate how easily Fitzgerald's profligacy and alcoholism – not to mention Zelda's mental illness – invite sensationalism.[20] To appreciate the kinky extremes to which many biographers now go, one need only compare Bruccoli's admittedly dry recitation of Fitzgerald's 1926 earnings – "His income for the year had reached a new high of $29,757.87 after commissions – including $15,300 from five stories. His total book royalties were $153.23. He paid federal taxes of $1,330.29" (*Epic Grandeur* 307) – to the purple prose that Jeffrey Meyers conjures up when addressing his subject's foot fetish:

> Though revolted by his own feet, he was sexually excited by the feet of women. His fearful associations with feet – which stuck out stiffly and were strongly associated with sex – both displaced and expressed his adolescent and adult fears about his masculinity. His deep-rooted insecurity later led him to seek embarrassing reassurance, not only from his mistresses of the 1930s but also from personal friends, about the size and potency of his sexual organ.[21]

Toes may be more salacious than taxes, but the figures that Bruccoli supplies are far more useful for understanding Fitzgerald's writing than any podiatric perversities he may have suffered in private.

Biography is by far the most prolific branch of contemporary criticism, with upwards of a dozen full-length volumes devoted to Scott's and Zelda's life together (not including various reminiscences by friends and acquaintances). Within this field one encounters the most contested issue concerning the couple – namely, the nature of their marriage and how it affected their work. In response to the unflattering portraits of Zelda in Mizener and Andrew Turnbull's *Scott Fitzgerald* (1962), Nancy Milford produced a revisionary portrait in her bestselling *Zelda* (1970), which emphasized the degree to which Zelda's own artistic inclinations, whether in writing, ballet, or painting, were stifled. Subsequent biographies such as Sally Cline's *Zelda Fitzgerald: Her Voice in Paradise* (2002) and Linda Wagner-Martin's *Zelda Sayre Fitzgerald: An American Woman's Life* (2004) have likewise prompted ire for depicting Scott as an abusive spouse who contributed to his wife's breakdown by belittling her talents. The extent to which they overcompensate for Zelda's public image as an unstable, immature Southern belle is best left to the reader's individual judgment; suffice it to say that most scholars recognize that the Fitzgeralds' marriage was complicated and fraught with mutual dependency and resentment, something vividly illustrated in the best primary source for assessing their relationship, Jackson R. Bryer's and Cathy W. Barks's *Dear Scott/Dearest Zelda: The Love Letters of F. Scott and Zelda Fitzgerald* (2002).

Concerns about Zelda's frustrated artistry reflect the rise of feminist studies. Two other political issues often lumped together with gender – race and class – have proved far less controversial. Given Fitzgerald's fixation with upward mobility, it is surprising that commentary on the latter remains fairly scattershot. To date, we lack a book-length study of Fitzgerald's ambivalence toward materialism, yet an excellent introduction to his economic ideals can be found in Scott Donaldson's essay "Possessions in *The Great Gatsby*" (2001), which examines how Jay Gatsby's ostentation is indicative of the "conspicuous consumption" and "pecuniary emulation" that Thorstein Veblen warned against in his landmark *Theory of the Leisure Class* (1899). Donaldson's piece should be read alongside my "Fitzgerald's Consumer World" in *A Historical Guide to F. Scott Fitzgerald* (2004), which demonstrates that Fitzgerald's fiction echoes not only Veblen but also his opponents, including the progressivist economist Stuart Patten, whose *The New Basis of Civilization* (1907) insisted that materialism served as a civilizing influence by offering the working and middle classes luxuries once reserved for aristocracies.[22]

As for race, the most vigorously contested issue is Fitzgerald's treatment of Jews. As early as 1947, Milton Hindus in *Commentary* objected to the "literary anti-Semitism" tainting the characterization of the gangster Meyer Wolfsheim in *The Great Gatsby*. William Goldhurst repeated the charge fifteen years later in *Congress Bi-Weekly*, inspiring a heated debate in the *Fitzgerald Newsletter* with Barry Gross, who claimed that Fitzgerald was caricaturing the gangster, not his ethnicity. Although Wolfsheim and other Jewish figures such as movie producer Joseph Bloeckman in *The Beautiful and Damned* are still occasionally dismissed as "racist" portraits, most critics agree with Gross, whose 1996 essay "What Fitzgerald Thought of the Jews: Resisting Type in 'The Hotel Child'" (co-authored with Eric Fretz) deserves the last word: "There is little [direct] evidence that Fitzgerald was concerned with the Jews, but his fiction reveals a man who sympathized and maybe even empathized with what it meant to be a Jew."[23]

Alas, the same cannot be said of his treatment of African-Americans, as the "darkie" minister in "The Camel's Back" testifies. With the exception of Robert Forrey's "Negroes in the Fiction of F. Scott Fitzgerald" (1967), however, the topic has not inspired objections like Hindus's and Goldhurst's. Instead, critics address more metaphorical figurations of race. In her essay "White Skin, White Mask: Passing, Posing, and Performing in *The Great Gatsby*" (2003), Meredith Goldsmith draws parallels between Gatsby's self-invention and the black tradition of "passing" as white in works such as James Weldon Johnson's *Autobiography of an Ex-Colored Man* (1912).[24] Such arguments are valuable because they remind us that racial assimilation was a defining issue in the 1920s. They also encourage us to read Fitzgerald alongside the contemporaneous Harlem Renaissance movement, with which he had little affiliation (or little interest in, apparently).[25] Yet such essays do not necessarily illuminate Fitzgerald's stance on racial matters, which was more complex than his casual use of stereotypes and epithets ("nigger" and "buck") would indicate. As Alan Margolies argues in "The Maturing of F. Scott Fitzgerald" (1997), "An obvious response is not to excuse [his racial prejudices] but to suggest that the United States during the writer's lifetime was racist . . . and, further, that Fitzgerald was not the only major writer of the time to employ [stereotypes]." At the same time, it is also important to recognize that Fitzgerald deprecated various theories of racial superiority, particularly Nordicism, which *Gatsby* lampoons through Tom Buchanan's convoluted ethnic pronouncements. Stories like "Two for a Cent" (1922) and "The Dance" (1926) also register Fitzgerald's objections to lynching – albeit fleetingly – noting that violent responses to changing race relations did far more to erode civilization than the "rising tide" of non-Caucasians ever could.[26]

Fitzgerald has not been as subject to the other dominant trend in post-1960s literary criticism, the bent for critical theory. His lyricism resists the deconstructive readings popularized by Jacques Derrida (1930–2004). Similarly, among competing schools such as Marxism, reader-response, and New Historicism, only psychoanalysis has proved popular – not surprising, perhaps, given that psychoanalysis is a major theme of *Tender Is the Night*. The methodology with the most potential for revealing unappreciated aspects of Fitzgerald is cultural studies, which looks to artifacts from film to fashion to advertising to understand the ways in which cultural media function as models of identity for consumers.

One groundbreaking study that falls into this category is Ronald Berman's The Great Gatsby *and Modern Times* (1994). The book sent a shock of excitement through scholars who presumed that *The Great Gatsby* had been thoroughly plumbed. Yet *Modern Times* is a wholly original reading because it seizes upon seemingly tangential textual details to reconstruct the era's popular culture. Thus Tom Buchanan's racist rants provide an opportunity to analyze the racist essays that routinely appeared in the *Saturday Evening Post*, while Daisy's ideals of love invite a discussion of the romance plots of silent movies. Even more intriguing, Berman explores how *Gatsby*'s narrative style parallels early cinematic techniques and how "the language of technology becomes absorbed in [its] tactics."[27] Berman has since published four additional volumes, including The Great Gatsby *and the World of Ideas* (1997), which once and for all debunks Wilson's claims that Fitzgerald was not an intellectual. As Berman demonstrates, *Gatsby* channels debates on class and identity of such influential 1920s thinkers as John Dewey (1859–1952), George Santayana (1863–1952), and Walter Lippmann (1889–1974).

Berman's method might best be compared with archeology: it attempts to excavate jewels of thought from the near-century's worth of sediment that separates us from the 1920s. A historical orientation is also evident in two recent essay collections, Ruth Prigozy's *The Cambridge Companion to F. Scott Fitzgerald* (2001) and my *A Historical Guide to F. Scott Fitzgerald*. Whether examining celebrity, youth culture, professionalism, the film industry, or the after effects of World War I, these efforts present either new or revisionary contexts for study that reveal the breadth of Fitzgerald's concerns. This project is also the mission of the recently founded *F. Scott Fitzgerald Review* (2002–), which takes an ecumenical approach to criticism, publishing autobiographical reminiscences, textual studies, and cultural inquiries. Topics of traditional interest have not been exhausted, however. As the popularity of Scott Donaldson's *Hemingway vs. Fitzgerald: The Rise and Fall of a Literary Friendship* (1999) attests, readers remain fascinated by the contentious competition between these two authors. Similarly, the national press coverage generated by James L. W. West III's *The Perfect Hour: The Romance of F. Scott Fitzgerald and Ginevra King, His First*

Love (2005), a portrait of the woman whose influence on *The Great Gatsby* rivals Zelda's, reflects a seemingly unquenchable appetite for new biographical insight. (Novelistic treatments are another sign of this continued fascination, Caroline Preston's *Gatsby's Girl* [2006] – which is little more than a reimagining of West's book in fictional form – attracted a great deal of attention, none of which focused on the novel's quality – merely its backstory.)

If one were to predict the future direction of Fitzgerald studies, it will probably be an effort to trace his historical import beyond the 1920s. How, we might ask, has his depiction of the romantic rituals of the Jazz Age influenced ideals of love and marriage in subsequent decades? What role has his notorious disdain for Hollywood had in depictions of the film industry since the 1930s? How do ongoing debates about the nature of his alcoholism and Zelda's mental illness reflect changing perceptions of those diseases? What, finally, can his conflicted dealings with the commercial fiction market teach us about the place of literature in the twenty-first century?

Such questions represent just a few potential avenues of inquiry. As the unabated interest in Fitzgerald over the past half-century suggests, his writing is notable for its capacity to remain relevant despite the shifting literary tastes that, regrettably, have diminished the stature of less fortunate contemporaries such as Thomas Wolfe (1900–1938) and John Steinbeck (1902–1968). Fitzgerald will remain a much-studied and much-taught author for at least two simple but important reasons: his themes tap into the human desire to transcend social boundaries to ambition and fulfillment, and his gorgeous style is without argument the most elegant and eloquent in American literary history.

Notes

Preface

1. "F. Scott Fitzgerald," *The Columbia Encyclopedia*, 6th edn (New York: Columbia University Press, 2001–5). http://www.bartleby.com/65/fi/FitzgS.html.
2. Since 1993, properly citing this book has proved problematic, given that Matthew J. Bruccoli in the Cambridge edition of the novel argued that *The Love of the Last Tycoon: A Western* was Fitzgerald's intended title. Most scholars continue to refer to it as *The Last Tycoon*.

Introduction

1. Azar Nafisi, *Reading Lolita in Tehran: A Memoir in Books* (New York: Random House, 2003), p. 127. Subsequent references cited parenthetically.
2. Scott Donaldson, *Hemingway vs. Fitzgerald: The Rise and Fall of a Literary Friendship* (Woodstock, NY: Overlook Press, 1999), pp. 299–300.
3. Nick Tosches, *King of the Jews* (New York: Ecco Press, 2005), pp. 168–9.
4. F. Scott Fitzgerald, *The Great Gatsby*, ed. Matthew J. Bruccoli (New York: Cambridge University Press, 1991), p. 2.
5. Ernest Hemingway, *A Moveable Feast* (New York: Scribner's, 1964), p. 174.
6. F. Scott Fitzgerald, *F. Scott Fitzgerald: A Life in Letters*, ed. Matthew J. Bruccoli (New York: Scribner's, 1994), p. 169.
7. F. Scott Fitzgerald, "The Swimmers," in *The Short Stories of F. Scott Fitzgerald: A New Collection*, ed. Matthew J. Bruccoli (New York: Scribner's, 1989), p. 512.

1 Life

1. F. Scott Fitzgerald, "Who's Who - - And Why," in *Afternoon of an Author: A Selection of Uncollected Stories and Essays*, ed. Arthur Mizener (New York: Scribner's, 1958), p. 83. Subsequent references to works in this collection cited parenthetically.
2. F. Scott Fitzgerald, *F. Scott Fitzgerald's Ledger: A Facsimile*, intro. Matthew J. Bruccoli (Washington, DC: NCR Microcard Books/Bruccoli Clark, 1973), pp. 178, 183, 192. Subsequent references cited parenthetically.

3. F. Scott Fitzgerald, "Sleeping and Waking," in *The Crack-Up*, ed. Edmund Wilson (New York: New Directions, 1945), p. 67. Subsequent references to works in this collection cited parenthetically.

4. John Chapin Mosher, "That Sad Young Man," in Matthew J. Bruccoli and Jackson R. Bryer, eds., *F. Scott Fitzgerald in His Own Time* (Kent, OH: Kent University Press, 1971), p. 443. Subsequent references to works in this collection cited parenthetically.

5. See, respectively, F. Scott Fitzgerald, *The Letters of F. Scott Fitzgerald*, ed. Andrew Turnbull (New York: Scribner's, 1964), p. 199, and "The Death of My Father," in *The Apprentice Fiction of F. Scott Fitzgerald*, ed. John Kuehl (New Brunswick: Rutgers University Press, 1965), p. 179. Subsequent references to both of these works cited parenthetically.

6. *Correspondence of F. Scott Fitzgerald*, ed. Matthew J. Bruccoli and Margaret M. Duggan (New York: Random House, 1980), p. 420. Subsequent references cited parenthetically.

7. F. Scott Fitzgerald, *A Life in Letters*, ed. Matthew J. Bruccoli (New York: Scribner's, 1994), p. 138. Subsequent references cited parenthetically.

8. F. Scott Fitzgerald, *This Side of Paradise*, ed. James L. W. West III (New York: Cambridge University Press, 1995), p. 24. Subsequent references cited parenthetically.

9. Patricia Hampl, Introduction to F. Scott Fitzgerald, *The St Paul Stories of F. Scott Fitzgerald*, ed. Patricia Hampl and Dave Page (St Paul: Borealis Books, 2004), p. xvii.

10. André LeVot, *F. Scott Fitzgerald*, trans. William Byron (Garden City: Doubleday, 1983), p. 10.

11. Arthur Mizener, *The Far Side of Paradise* (Boston: Houghton Mifflin, 1951), p. 48. Subsequent references cited parenthetically.

12. Glenway Wescott, quoted in Scott Donaldson, *Fool for Love* (New York: Congdon & Weed, 1983), p. 23.

13. F. Scott Fitzgerald, *The Notebooks of F. Scott Fitzgerald*, ed. Matthew J. Bruccoli (New York: Harcourt Brace Jovanovich/Bruccoli Clark, 1978), pp. 165–6. Subsequent references cited parenthetically.

14. James L. W. West III, *The Perfect Hour: The Romance of F. Scott Fitzgerald and Ginevra King, His First Love* (New York: Random House, 2005), p. xvi.

15. Zelda Fitzgerald, *Save Me the Waltz*, in *The Collected Writings of Zelda Fitzgerald*, ed. Matthew J. Bruccoli (New York: Scribner's, 1992), p. 32.

16. Ruth Prigozy, *F. Scott Fitzgerald* (London and New York: Penguin, 2001), pp. 36–7.

17. F. Scott Fitzgerald, "The Last of the Belles," in *The Short Stories of F. Scott Fitzgerald: A New Collection*, ed. Matthew J. Bruccoli (New York: Scribner's, 1989), p. 450. Subsequent references to stories in this collection cited parenthetically.

18. Quoted in Matthew J. Bruccoli, *Some Sort of Epic Grandeur: The Life of F. Scott Fitzgerald*, 1st rev. edn (New York: Carroll & Graf, 1991), pp. 624–5. Subsequent references cited parenthetically. The stories adapted for the movies were "Head and Shoulders" (retitled *The Chorus Girl's Romance*), "Myra Meets His Family" (retitled *The Husband Hunter*), and "The Offshore Pirate," all released in 1920. Unfortunately, none of these silent films survives.

19. Quoted in Nancy Milford, *Zelda: A Biography* (New York: Harper & Row, 1970), p. 79.

20. John Peale Bishop, "Mr. Fitzgerald Sees the Flapper Through," in Jackson R. Bryer, ed., *F. Scott Fitzgerald: The Critical Reception* (New York: Burt Franklin, 1978), p. 74. Subsequent references to reviews in this collection cited parenthetically.

21. F. Scott Fitzgerald, *Tales of the Jazz Age* (New York: Scribner's, 1922), p. xi.

22. Matthew J. Bruccoli, "Writing *The Great Gatsby*," in Matthew J. Bruccoli, ed., *F. Scott Fitzgerald's* The Great Gatsby: *A Literary Reference* (New York: Carroll & Graf, 2002), p. 76. Subsequent references cited parenthetically.

23. *Dear Scott/Dear Max: The Fitzgerald–Perkins Correspondence*, ed. John Kuehl and Jackson R. Bryer (London: Cassell, 1971), p. 84. Subsequent references cited parenthetically.

24. Ernest Hemingway, *A Moveable Feast* (New York: Scribner's, 1964), p. 190.

25. Sara Mayfield, *Exiles from Paradise: Zelda and Scott Fitzgerald* (New York: Delacorte, 1971), p. 141.

26. Scott Donaldson, *Hemingway vs. Fitzgerald: The Rise and Fall of a Literary Friendship* (Woodstock, NY: Overlook Press, 1999), p. 156.

27. Linda Wagner-Martin, *Zelda Sayre Fitzgerald: An American Woman's Life* (London: Praeger, 2004), pp. 136–7.

28. F. Scott Fitzgerald, "General Plan," in Matthew J. Bruccoli with Judith S. Baughman, *A Reader's Companion to F. Scott Fitzgerald's* Tender Is the Night (Columbia: University of South Carolina Press, 1996), p. 10.

29. O. O. McIntyre, "New York Day by Day," in *As Ever, Scott Fitz – : Letters Between F. Scott Fitzgerald and His Literary Agent, Harold Ober: 1919–1940*, ed. Matthew J. Bruccoli (Philadelphia: Lippincott, 1972), p. 253.

30. Sheilah Graham, *The Real F. Scott Fitzgerald Thirty-Five Years Later* (New York: Grosset & Dunlap, 1976), pp. 96–115. This book combines two earlier memoirs, *Beloved Infidel* (1958) and *College of One* (1967).

31. *Dear Scott/Dearest Zelda: The Love Letters of F. Scott and Zelda Fitzgerald*, ed. Jackson R. Bryer and Cathy W. Barks (New York: Scribner's, 2002), p. 382.

2 Cultural context

1. "Echoes of the Jazz Age," in *The Crack-Up*, ed. Edmund Wilson (New York: New Directions, 1945), pp. 14, 15. Subsequent references to works in this collection cited parenthetically.

2. "The Last of the Belles," in *The Short Stories of F. Scott Fitzgerald: A New Collection*, ed. Matthew J. Bruccoli (New York: Scribner's, 1989), p. 483. Subsequent references to stories in this collection cited parenthetically.

3. F. Scott Fitzgerald, *The Letters of F. Scott Fitzgerald*, ed. Andrew Turnbull (New York: Scribner's, 1964), p. 159–60. Subsequent references cited parenthetically.

4. F. Scott Fitzgerald, "The Author's Apology," in Matthew J. Bruccoli and Jackson R. Bryer, eds., *F. Scott Fitzgerald in His Own Time* (Kent, OH: Kent University Press,

1971), p. 164. Subsequent references to works in this collection cited parenthetically. For an overview of the rise of this cohort mindset, see Steven Mintz, *Huck's Raft: A History of American Childhood* (Cambridge, MA: Harvard University Press, 2004), pp. 213–32.

5. G. Stanley Hall, *Adolescence and Its Psychology and Its Relations to Physiology, Anthropology, Sociology, Sex, Crime, Religion, and Education*, 2 vols. (New York: Appleton, 1904), II, p. 59.

6. Arthur Mizener, *The Far Side of Paradise* (Boston: Houghton Mifflin, 1951), p. 93. Subsequent references cited parenthetically.

7. Samantha Barbas, *Movie Crazy: Fans, Stars, and the Cult of Celebrity* (London: Palgrave Macmillan, 2001), p. 42.

8. "The Unspeakable Egg," in *The Price Was High: The Last Uncollected Stories of F. Scott Fitzgerald*, ed. Matthew J. Bruccoli (New York: Harcourt Brace Jovanovich, 1979), p. 141. Subsequent references cited parenthetically.

9. Angela J. Latham, *Posing a Threat: Flappers, Chorus Girls, and Other Brazen Performers of the American 1920s* (Hanover, NH: Wesleyan University Press, 2000), pp. 19–20. Subsequent references cited parenthetically.

10. Paula S. Fass, *The Damned and the Beautiful: American Youth in the 1920s* (New York: Oxford University Press, 1977), p. 262. Subsequent references cited parenthetically.

11. F. Scott Fitzgerald, *The Great Gatsby*, ed. Matthew J. Bruccoli (New York: Cambridge University Press, 1991), p. 48. Subsequent references cited parenthetically.

12. F. Scott Fitzgerald, *Tender Is the Night* (New York: Scribner's, 1934), p. 16. Subsequent references cited parenthetically.

13. Stuart Ewen, *All Consuming Images: The Politics of Style in Contemporary Culture* (New York: Basic Books, 1988), p. 75. Subsequent references cited parenthetically.

14. F. Scott Fitzgerald, *This Side of Paradise*, ed. James L. W. West III (New York: Cambridge University Press, 1995), p. 18. Subsequent references cited parenthetically.

15. F. Scott Fitzgerald, "He Thinks He's Wonderful," in *The Basil and Josephine Stories*, ed. Jackson R. Bryer and John Kuehl (New York: Scribner's, 1973), p. 120. Subsequent references cited parenthetically.

16. Frederick Lewis Allen, *Only Yesterday: An Informal History of the 1920's* (New York: Wiley & Sons, 1997), p. 145.

17. Anthony J. Berret, "Basil and the Dance Craze," *The F. Scott Fitzgerald Review* 3 (2004), 88–107.

18. Nathan Miller, *New World Coming: The 1920s and the Making of Modern America* (New York: Scribner's, 2003), p. 261.

3 Works

1. F. Scott Fitzgerald, "One Hundred False Starts," in *Afternoon of an Author: A Selection of Uncollected Stories and Essays*, ed. Arthur Mizener (New York: Scribner's, 1958), p. 132. Subsequent references cited parenthetically.

2. James L. W. West III, "F. Scott Fitzgerald, Professional Author," in Kirk Curnutt, ed., *A Historical Guide to F. Scott Fitzgerald* (New York: Oxford University Press, 2004), p. 53. Subsequent references to essays in this collection cited parenthetically.

3. Matthew J. Bruccoli, *Some Sort of Epic Grandeur: The Life of F. Scott Fitzgerald*, 1st rev. edn (New York: Carroll & Graf, 1991), p. 142. Subsequent references cited parenthetically.

4. F. Scott Fitzgerald, *The Notebooks of F. Scott Fitzgerald*, ed. Matthew J. Bruccoli (New York: Harcourt Brace Jovanovich/Bruccoli Clark, 1978), p. 131. Subsequent references cited parenthetically.

5. Harvey Eagleton, "Prophets of the New Age: F. Scott Fitzgerald and *The Great Gatsby*," in Matthew J. Bruccoli and Jackson R. Bryer, eds., *F. Scott Fitzgerald in His Own Time* (Kent, OH: Kent University Press, 1971), p. 438. Subsequent references to works in this collection cited parenthetically.

6. André LeVot, *F. Scott Fitzgerald*, trans. William Byron (Garden City: Doubleday, 1983), p. 88.

7. F. Scott Fitzgerald, *A Life in Letters*, ed. Matthew J. Bruccoli (New York: Scribner's, 1994) p. 121. Subsequent references cited parenthetically.

8. F. Scott Fitzgerald, "'The Sensible Thing,'" in *The Short Stories of F. Scott Fitzgerald: A New Collection*, ed. Matthew J. Bruccoli (New York: Scribner's, 1989), p. 301. Subsequent references to stories in this collection cited parenthetically.

9. Alice Hall Petry, *Fitzgerald's Craft of Short Fiction: The Collected Stories, 1920–1935* (Tuscaloosa: University of Alabama Press, 1989), p. 140. Subsequent references cited parenthetically.

10. Linda Patterson Miller, ed., *Letters from the Lost Generation* (New Brunswick: Rutgers University Press, 1994), pp. 17–18.

11. *Correspondence of F. Scott Fitzgerald*, ed. Matthew J. Bruccoli and Margaret M. Duggan (New York: Random House, 1980), p. 671. Subsequent references cited parenthetically.

12. F. Scott Fitzgerald, *The Letters of F. Scott Fitzgerald*, ed. Andrew Turnbull (New York: Scribner's, 1964), p. 93. Subsequent references cited parenthetically.

13. *As Ever, Scott Fitz–: Letters Between F. Scott Fitzgerald and His Literary Agent, Harold Ober: 1919–1940*, ed. Matthew J. Bruccoli (Philadelphia: Lippincott, 1972), p. 384. Subsequent references cited parenthetically.

14. Ernest Hemingway, *A Moveable Feast* (New York: Scribner's, 1964), p. 156.

15. Bryant Mangum, "The Short Stories of F. Scott Fitzgerald," in Ruth Prigozy, ed., *The Cambridge Companion to F. Scott Fitzgerald* (New York: Cambridge University Press, 2001), p. 61. Subsequent references cited parenthetically.

16. F. Scott Fitzgerald, *The Great Gatsby* (New York: Cambridge University Press, 1991), p. 120. Subsequent references cited parenthetically.

17. F. Scott Fitzgerald, *Tender Is the Night* (New York: Scribner's, 1934), p. 143. Subsequent references cited parenthetically.

18. Matthew J. Bruccoli, *The Composition of* Tender Is the Night (Pittsburgh: University of Pittsburgh Press, 1963), p. 166. Subsequent references cited parenthetically.

19. R.V.A.S., review of *This Side of Paradise*, in Jackson R. Bryer, ed., *F. Scott Fitzgerald: The Critical Reception* (New York: Burt Franklin, 1978), p. 22. Subsequent references to reviews in this collection cited parenthetically.
20. F. Scott Fitzgerald, *The Beautiful and Damned* (New York: Scribner's, 1922), p. 278. Subsequent references cited parenthetically.
21. *Dear Scott/Dear Max: The Fitzgerald–Perkins Correspondence*, ed. John Kuehl and Jackson R. Bryer (London: Cassell, 1971), p. 50. Subsequent references cited parenthetically.
22. F. Scott Fitzgerald, *Trimalchio: An Early Version of* The Great Gatsby, ed. James L. W. West III (New York: Cambridge University Press, 2000), p. 117. Subsequent references cited parenthetically.
23. Quoted in Matthew J. Bruccoli with Judith S. Baughman, *A Reader's Companion to* Tender Is the Night (Columbia: University of South Carolina Press, 1996), pp. 6, 18. Subsequent references cited parenthetically.
24. Matthew J. Bruccoli, *"The Last of the Novelists": F. Scott Fitzgerald and* The Last Tycoon (Carbondale: Southern Illinois University Press, 1977), p. 129. Subsequent references cited parenthetically.
25. Frances Kroll Ring, *Against the Current: As I Remember F. Scott Fitzgerald* (San Francisco: David Ellis, 1987), p. 93.
26. F. Scott Fitzgerald, *The Love of the Last Tycoon: A Western*, ed. Matthew J. Bruccoli (New York: Cambridge University Press, 1993), p. 77. Subsequent references cited parenthetically.
27. F. Scott Fitzgerald, "Presumption," in *The Price Was High: The Last Uncollected Stories of F. Scott Fitzgerald*, ed. Matthew J. Bruccoli (New York: Harcourt Brace Jovanovich, 1979), p. 192. Subsequent references cited parenthetically.
28. F. Scott Fitzgerald, *This Side of Paradise*, ed. James L. West III (New York: Cambridge University Press, 1995), pp. 24, 88.
29. Ernest Hemingway, in *The Only Thing that Counts: The Ernest Hemingway–Maxwell Perkins Correspondence, 1925–1947*, ed. Matthew J. Bruccoli (Columbia: University of South Carolina Press, 1996), p. 209.
30. Arthur Mizener, *The Far Side of Paradise* (New York: Houghton Mifflin, 1951), pp. 214–15.
31. F. Scott Fitzgerald, "The Crack-Up," in *The Crack-Up*, ed. Edmund Wilson (New York: New Directions, 1945), p. 70. Subsequent references to works in this collection cited parenthetically.
32. "Family in the Wind," in *The Stories of F. Scott Fitzgerald*, ed. Malcolm Cowley (New York: Scribner's, 1951), pp. 426, 435. Subsequent references cited parenthetically.
33. John W. Crowley, *The White Logic: Alcoholism and Gender in Modernist Fiction* (Amherst: University of Massachusetts Press, 1995), p. 69.
34. F. Scott Fitzgerald, "Gretchen's Forty Winks," in *All the Sad Young Men* (New York: Scribner's, 1926), p. 247. Subsequent references to stories in this collection cited parenthetically.

35. Judith Fetterley, *The Resisting Reader: A Feminist Approach to Modern Fiction* (Bloomington: Indiana University Press, 1972), p. xvi.

36. Ronald Berman, The Great Gatsby *and Modern Times* (Urbana: University of Illinois Press, 1994), p. 121. Subsequent references cited parenthetically.

37. F. Scott Fitzgerald, "Dalyrimple Goes Wrong," in *Before Gatsby: The First Twenty-Six Stories*, ed. Matthew J. Bruccoli (Columbia: University of South Carolina Press, 2002), p. 72. Subsequent references to stories in this collection cited parenthetically.

38. Henry Dan Piper, *F. Scott Fitzgerald: A Critical Portrait* (Carbondale: Southern Illinois University Press, 1965), p. 271.

39. "Basil and Cleopatra," in *The Basil and Josephine Stories*, ed. Jackson R. Bryer and John Kuehl (New York: Scribner's, 1973), p. 222. Subsequent references cited parenthetically.

40. Scott Donaldson, *Fool for Love* (New York: Congdon & Weed, 1983), p. 101.

41. Richard Lehan, *F. Scott Fitzgerald and the Craft of Fiction* (Carbondale: University of Southern Illinois Press, 1966), p. 80.

42. J. Gerald Kennedy, *Imagining Paris: Exile, Writing, and American Identity* (New Haven: Yale University Press, 1993), p. 203.

43. Andrew Turnbull, *Scott Fitzgerald* (New York: Scribner's, 1962), p. 295.

44. F. Scott Fitzgerald, *The Pat Hobby Stories*, ed. Arnold Gingrich (New York: Scribner's, 1962), p. 22. Subsequent references to stories in this collection cited parenthetically.

45. Bryant Mangum, *A Fortune Yet: Money in the Art of F. Scott Fitzgerald's Short Stories* (New York: Garland, 1991), p. 28.

46. Lionel Trilling, "F. Scott Fitzgerald," in Arthur Mizener, ed., *F. Scott Fitzgerald: A Collection of Critical Essays* (Englewood Cliffs, NJ: Prentice-Hall, 1963), p. 12.

47. Lawrence Buell, "The Significance of Fantasy in Fitzgerald's Short Fiction," in Jackson R. Bryer, ed., *The Short Stories of F. Scott Fitzgerald: New Approaches in Criticism* (Madison: University of Wisconsin Press, 1982), p. 34.

48. Ezra Pound, *Hugh Selwyn Mauberley*, in *The Selected Poems of Ezra Pound* (New York: New Directions, 1957), p. 64.

49. T. S. Eliot, *The Waste Land*, in *The Complete Poems and Plays, 1909–1950* (New York: Harcourt, Brace, & World, 1971), p. 38. Subsequent references cited parenthetically.

50. Robert Sklar, *F. Scott Fitzgerald: The Last Laocoön* (New York: Oxford University Press, 1967), pp. 104–5.

51. Milton R. Stern, "Fitzgerald's Last Style," in Jackson R. Bryer, Ruth Prigozy, and Milton R. Stern, eds., *F. Scott Fitzgerald in the Twenty-First Century* (Tuscaloosa: University of Alabama Press, 2003), pp. 319, 329.

4 Critical reception

1. Jackson R. Bryer, ed., *F. Scott Fitzgerald: The Critical Reception* (New York: Burt Franklin, 1978), pp. 1–32. Subsequent references to reviews in this collection cited parenthetically.

2. Edmund Wilson, *Letters on Literature and Politics 1912–1972*, ed. Elena Wilson (New York: Farrar, Straus, & Giroux, 1977), p. 46.
3. Jeffrey Meyers, *Edmund Wilson: A Biography* (New York: Houghton Mifflin, 1995), p. 53. Subsequent references cited parenthetically.
4. Edmund Wilson, "Literary Spotlight," in Matthew J. Bruccoli and Jackson R. Bryer, eds., *F. Scott Fitzgerald in His Own Time* (Kent, OH: Kent University Press, 1971), p. 404. Subsequent references cited parenthetically.
5. "I congratulate you – you have succeeded here in doing most of the things that people have always scolded you for not doing," Wilson wrote to Fitzgerald. See Wilson, *Letters on Literature*, p. 121.
6. Fitzgerald, by contrast, never lost respect for Wilson's critical acumen; in his *Crack-Up* essays he identifies him as his "intellectual conscience." See F. Scott Fitzgerald, *The Crack-Up*, ed. Edmund Wilson (New York: New Directions, 1945), p. 79.
7. Matthew J. Bruccoli, *Some Sort of Epic Grandeur: The Life of F. Scott Fitzgerald*, 1st rev. edn (New York: Carroll & Graf, 1991), pp. 55–6. Subsequent references cited parenthetically.
8. H. L. Mencken, *My Life as Author and Editor*, ed. Jonathan Yardley (New York: Random House, 1993), p. 265.
9. Hans Bak, *Malcolm Cowley: The Formative Years* (Athens: University of Georgia Press, 1993), p. 464.
10. Malcolm Cowley, "The Double Man," *Saturday Review of Literature* 34 (February 14, 1951), 9.
11. Jackson R. Bryer, "The Critical Reputation of F. Scott Fitzgerald," in Ruth Prigozy, ed., *The Cambridge Companion to F. Scott Fitzgerald* (New York: Cambridge University Press, 2001), p. 211. Subsequent references cited parenthetically.
12. Malcolm Cowley, "Of Clocks and Calendars," *New Republic* 104 (March 17, 1941), 376; John Dos Passos, "A Note on Fitzgerald," in Fitzgerald, *The Crack-Up*, p. 339.
13. Arthur Mizener, "F. Scott Fitzgerald – Moralist of the Jazz Age," *Harper's Bazaar* 83 (September 1949), 174.
14. See Arthur Mizener, ed., *F. Scott Fitzgerald: A Collection of Critical Essays* (Englewood Cliffs, NJ: Prentice-Hall, 1963). pp. 12, 16, 33, and 125 respectively.
15. Most of these essays are collected either in Mizener, *F. Scott Fitzgerald: A Collection of Critical Essays*, or Ernest Lockridge, ed., *Twentieth Century Interpretations of The Great Gatsby* (Englewood Cliffs, NJ: Prentice-Hall, 1968).
16. James E. Miller, Jr., *F. Scott Fitzgerald: His Art and Technique* (New York: New York University Press, 1964), pp. 2, 135.
17. Milton R. Stern, *The Golden Moment: The Novels of F. Scott Fitzgerald* (Urbana: University of Illinois Press, 1970).
18. Matthew J. Bruccoli, *The Composition of Tender Is the Night* (Pittsburgh: University of Pittsburgh Press, 1963), pp. 3, xiv.
19. Matthew J. Bruccoli, General Introduction to *F. Scott Fitzgerald: Manuscripts*, ed. Bruccoli (New York: Garland, 1990–1), p. ix. See also Bruccoli, "The Writing of *The Great Gatsby*," in Bruccoli, ed., *F. Scott Fitzgerald's* The Great Gatsby: *A Literary*

Reference (New York: Carroll & Graf, 2002), and *"The Last of the Novelists": F. Scott Fitzgerald and* The Last Tycoon (Carbondale: Southern Illinois University Press, 1977).

20. *Invented Lives* is especially disappointing given that Mellow authored sterling biographies of Gertrude Stein (1973), Ernest Hemingway (1992), and Walker Evans (1999).

21. Jeffrey Meyers, *F. Scott Fitzgerald: A Biography* (New York: HarperCollins, 1994), p. 14.

22. Scott Donaldson, "Possessions in *The Great Gatsby*," in Harold Bloom, ed., *The Great Gatsby – F. Scott Fitzgerald* (New York: Chelsea House, 2003), pp. 185–207, and Kirk Curnutt, "Fitzgerald's Consumer World," in Curnutt, ed., *A Historical Guide to F. Scott Fitzgerald* (New York: Oxford University Press, 2004), pp. 85–128.

23. Barry Gross and Eric Fretz, "What Fitzgerald Thought of the Jews: Resisting Type in 'The Hotel Child,'" in Jackson R. Bryer, ed., *New Essays on F. Scott Fitzgerald's Neglected Stories* (Columbia: University of Missouri Press, 1996), p. 192.

24. Meredith Goldsmith, "White Skin, White Mask: Passing, Posing, and Performance in *The Great Gatsby*," *Modern Fiction Studies* 49 (Fall 2003), 443; see also Robert Forrey, "Negroes in the Fiction of F. Scott Fitzgerald," *Phylon* 28:3 (1967), 293–8.

25. The fact that Fitzgerald admired Carl Van Vechten's popular novel *Nigger Heaven* (1925), which celebrated the supposed primitivism of black life, is not necessarily an indication of racism; a number of Harlem Renaissance writers, including Langston Hughes and Wallace Thurman, also commended the book.

26. Alan Margolies, "The Maturing of F. Scott Fitzgerald," *Twentieth-Century Literature* 43 (Spring 1997), 74, 91.

27. Ronald Berman, The Great Gatsby *and Modern Times* (Urbana: University of Illinois Press, 1994), p. 137. See also Berman's *Fitzgerald, Hemingway, and the Twenties* (Tuscaloosa: University of Alabama Press, 2002); *Fitzgerald–Hemingway–Wilson: Language and Experience* (Tuscaloosa: University of Alabama Press, 2003); and *Modernity and Progress: Fitzgerald, Hemingway, Orwell* (Tuscaloosa: University of Alabama Press, 2005).

Guide to further reading

F. Scott Fitzgerald: key editions

This Side of Paradise. 1920. Ed. James L. W. West III (Cambridge and New York: Cambridge University Press, 1995).

Flappers and Philosophers. 1920. Ed James L. W. West III (Cambridge and New York: Cambridge University Press, 1999).

The Beautiful and Damned (New York: Scribner's, 1922).

Tales of the Jazz Age. 1922. Ed. James L. W. West III (Cambridge and New York: Cambridge University Press, 2002).

The Vegetable (New York: Scribner's, 1923).

The Great Gatsby. 1925. Ed. Matthew J. Bruccoli (Cambridge and New York: Cambridge University Press, 1991).

All the Sad Young Men. 1926. Ed. James L. W. West III (Cambridge and New York: Cambridge University Press, 2007).

Tender Is the Night (New York: Scribner's, 1934).

Taps at Reveille (New York: Scribner's, 1935).

The Last Tycoon. 1941. Republished as *The Love of the Last Tycoon: A Western.* Ed. Matthew J. Bruccoli (Cambridge and New York: Cambridge University Press, 1993).

The Crack-Up. Ed. Edmund Wilson (New York: New Directions, 1945).

Afternoon of an Author. Ed. Arthur Mizener (New York: Scribner's, 1958).

The Pat Hobby Stories. Ed. Arnold Gingrich (New York: Scribner's, 1962).

The Basil and Josephine Stories. Ed. Jackson R. Bryer and John Kuehl (New York: Scribner's, 1973).

The Short Stories of F. Scott Fitzgerald: A New Collection. Ed. Matthew J. Bruccoli (New York: Scribner's, 1989).

Trimalchio: An Early Version of The Great Gatsby. Ed. James L. W. West III (Cambridge and New York: Cambridge University Press, 2000).

Secondary sources

The following list includes studies not cited in depth in preceding chapters. For optimal accessibility, these recommendations are limited to secondary sources currently in print.

Baughman, Judith S., with Matthew J. Bruccoli. *Literary Masters: F. Scott Fitzgerald* (New York: Gale, 2000).
An informative introduction designed for high school and undergraduate students. Part of the Gale Studies Guide to Great Literature series.

Berman, Ronald. *Fitzgerald, Hemingway, and the Twenties* (Tuscaloosa: University of Alabama Press, 2002).
—. *Fitzgerald–Hemingway–Wilson: Language and Experience* (Tuscaloosa: University of Alabama Press, 2003).
—. The Great Gatsby *and Fitzgerald's World of Ideas* (Tuscaloosa: University of Alabama Press, 1997).
—. *Modernity and Progress: Fitzgerald, Hemingway, Orwell* (Tuscaloosa: University of Alabama Press, 2005).
These follow-ups to Berman's The Great Gatsby *and Modern Times* are not always as accessible as that essential study, yet their inquiries into such important 1920s themes as American optimism, language, and Freudian sexuality give overdue consideration to Fitzgerald's philosophical subtexts. Especially interesting for their choice of proof texts, which include such seemingly self-explanatory efforts as "Bernice Bobs Her Hair" and "The Third Casket."

Bloom, Harold. Ed. *F. Scott Fitzgerald* (Philadelphia: Chelsea House, 1999).
An entry in the Bloom's Major Short Story Writers series. Offers background and criticism on "May Day," "The Diamond as Big as the Ritz," "Babylon Revisited," and, curiously, "Crazy Sunday."

—. *F. Scott Fitzgerald's* The Great Gatsby (Philadelphia: Chelsea House, 2004).
Offers a sampling of recent criticism of the novel, with topics ranging from Nick Carraway as narrator to literary sources such as *Troilus and Criseyde.* Includes Scott Donaldson's excellent "Possessions in *The Great Gatsby.*"

Bruccoli, Matthew J. Ed. *F. Scott Fitzgerald's* The Great Gatsby: *A Literary Reference* (New York: Carroll & Graf, 2002).
Provides background on *Gatsby's* characters and setting, as well as a selection of reviews and criticism. Most valuable for its second chapter, a revision of Bruccoli's 1973 composition history of the novel.

—. *Some Sort of Epic Grandeur: The Life of F. Scott Fitzgerald.* 1st rev. edn (New York Carroll & Graf 1991).
The most reliable of the dozen-plus extant biographies. Essential for any study of Fitzgerald.

—, and George Anderson. *F. Scott Fitzgerald's Tender Is the Night: A Documentary Volume* (Detroit: Gale, 2003).
Volume 273 of Gale's Dictionary of Literary Biography series. A somewhat more scholarly and expanded version of the *Reader's Companion* (see below).

—, with Judith S. Baughman. *A Reader's Companion to F. Scott Fitzgerald's* Tender Is the Night (Columbia: University of South Carolina Press, 1996).

Most valuable for its concise overview of *Tender*'s tortured composition
history, Bruccoli's explanatory notes, and George Anderson's comprehensive
list of the short story "strippings" that Fitzgerald incorporated into the novel.

Bryer, Jackson R. *New Essays on F. Scott Fitzgerald's Neglected Stories* (Columbia:
     University of Missouri Press, 1996).
Important for calling attention to oft-ignored stories such as "Dalyrimple Goes
Wrong" and "The Curious Case of Benjamin Button," emphasizing the atypical
traditions within which Fitzgerald dabbled, including fantasy and mystery.

—, Alan Margolies, and Ruth Prigozy. *F. Scott Fitzgerald: New Perspectives*
     (Athens: University of Georgia Press, 2000).
Essays from the first Fitzgerald Society conference at Hofstra University in 1992,
with excellent essays on *The Last Tycoon*, the Philippe stories, and "Outside the
Cabinet-Maker's." Also includes compelling reminiscences by Budd Schulberg,
Frances Kroll Ring, and Charles Scribner III.

—, Ruth Prigozy, and Milton R. Stern. *F. Scott Fitzgerald in the Twenty-First
     Century* (Tuscaloosa: University of Alabama Press, 2003).
A wide-ranging essay collection from the centennial celebrations at Princeton
University in 1996. Offers insight into many lesser-known works, including *The
Beautiful and Damned*, *Basil and Josephine*, and the Pat Hobby stories.

Canterbury, E. Ray, and Thomas Birch. *F. Scott Fitzgerald: Under the Influence*
     (New York: Paragon House, 2006).
An economics-based overview of Fitzgerald's career that explores the boom
mentality of the 1920s and its effect on consumerism and popular culture.

Curnutt, Kirk. Ed. *A Historical Guide to F. Scott Fitzgerald* (New York: Oxford
     University Press, 2004).
Essay collection examining the historical contexts of Fitzgerald's life and work.
Topics include professionalism, intellectual backgrounds, consumerism, flapper
films, and war.

DeKoster, Katie. Ed. *Readings on F. Scott Fitzgerald* (San Diego: Greenhaven Press,
     1998).
A serviceable if brief collection of Fitzgerald criticism. Includes an excellent
little-known essay by Sven Birkets ("A Gatsby for Today").

Donaldson, Scott. *Hemingway vs. Fitzgerald: The Rise and Fall of a Literary
     Friendship* (Woodstock, NY: Overlook Press, 1999).
The most comprehensive overview of the rivals' fractious relationship. Compares
their treatment of love and rejection, fame, alcoholism, and expatriation.

Gross, Dalton, and MaryJean Gross. *Understanding* The Great Gatsby (Westport,
     CT: Greenwood Press, 1998).
Offers contextual analysis of the book, focusing on such period themes as
scandals, money, and women's liberation.

Hook, Andrew. *F. Scott Fitzgerald: A Literary Life* (London: Palgrave, 2002).
A biographical study focusing on the conflict between Fitzgerald's
"tender-minded" and "tough-minded" impulses, the former accounting for his
moral sensibility and the second for his ambition.

Kennedy, J. Gerald. *Imagining Paris: Exile, Writing, and American Identity* (New
Haven: Yale University Press, 1993).
Explores major 1920s expatriate works, including *Tender Is the Night*, focusing on
the displacement and identity crises that accompany living abroad.

—, and Jackson R. Bryer. Eds. *French Connections: Hemingway and Fitzgerald
Abroad* (New York: St. Martin's Press, 1998).
An essay collection focusing on Hemingway's and Fitzgerald's expatriate years.
Includes several excellent entries on *Tender Is the Night*.

Kuehl, John. *F. Scott Fitzgerald: A Study of the Short Fiction* (Boston: Twayne,
1991).
An informative study of Fitzgerald's stories, from apprentice efforts to
posthumous collections. Also provides an overview of the stories' critical
reception, including excerpts from both contemporary reviewers and subsequent
scholars.

Lehan, Richard D. The Great Gatsby: *The Limits of Wonder* (Boston: Twayne,
1990).
A solid introduction to *Gatsby*, focusing on the themes of romance and money.

Prigozy, Ruth. *F. Scott Fitzgerald* (New York and London: Penguin, 2001).
An accessible biography featuring dozens of rare photographs. Part of Penguin's
Illustrated Lives series.

Ed. *The Cambridge Companion to F. Scott Fitzgerald* (New York: Cambridge
University Press, 2001).
Includes essays on celebrity, youth culture, expatriation, Fitzgerald's non-fiction,
and female characters, as well as analyses of *Gatsby* and *Tender*. Valuable for
Jackson R. Bryer's essential overview of Fitzgerald's reception history.

Stern, Milton R. Tender Is the Night: *The Broken Universe* (Boston: Twayne, 1994).
An introduction to the novel, focusing on World War I's effect on mores and
character.

Tate, Mary Jo. *F. Scott Fitzgerald: A to Z* (New York: Checkmark Books, 1998).
An encyclopedic reference guide, with entries on major peers, characters, works,
and themes.

West, James L. W. III. *The Perfect Hour: The Romance of F. Scott Fitzgerald and
Ginevra King, His First Love* (New York: Random House, 2005).
The most detailed discussion to date of Fitzgerald's first love and her influence on
stories such as "Winter Dreams." Includes excerpts from previously unpublished

letters and diaries, as well as a 1916 short story that King wrote in response to Fitzgerald's wooing.

Zeitz, Joshua. *Flapper: A Madcap Story of Sex, Style, Celebrity, and the Women Who Made America Modern* (New York: Crown, 2006).
A lively history of the flapper subculture that compares Scott's and Zelda's writings on modern womanhood to other era emblems such as fashion designer Coco Chanel, actress Clara Bow, and *New Yorker* columnist Lois Long.

Index